owac

A PILGRIM'S GUIDE TO THE
Camino Sanabrés
Ourense – A Laxe – Santiago
&
Camino Invierno
Ponferrada – A Laxe – Santiago

D0872869

*A Practical & Mystical Manual
for the Modern-day Pilgrim*

John Brierley

First edition published in 2021

ISBN: 978-1-912216-21-5 (print)
ISBN: 978-1-912216-90-1 (mobi)
ISBN: 978-1-912216-91-8 (epub)

British Library Cataloguing-in-Publication Data.
A catalogue record for this book is available from the British Library.

Printed and bound in the European Union

Published by

CAMINO GUIDES
An imprint of Kaminn Media Ltd
272 Bath Street,
Glasgow, G2 4JR

Tel: +44(0)141 354 1758
Fax: +44(0)141 354 1759

Email: info@caminoguides.com
Web: _www.caminoguides.com_

Cover photograph: _Camino Invierno – Las Médulas (World Heritage Site)_

Ourense – Santiago: 1–5 *Camino Sanabrés*

Ponferrada – Santiago: 01 – 08 *Camino Invierno*

MAP LEGEND: Symbols & Abbreviations

Total km *equiv.*	Total distance for stage
	Adj. for climb (100m vertical =+ 0.5 km effort =+ 10 minutes)
(850m) Alto ▲	Contours / High point of each stage
< Ⓐ Ⓗ >	Intermediate accommodation (*often less busy / quieter*)
◄ 3.5	Precise distance between points (3.5 km = ± 1 hour)
―● 50m > / ^ / <	Interim distances 50m right> / s/o=straight on^ / <left

	Natural path / forest track / gravel *senda*
	Quiet country lane (asphalt)
	Secondary road (*grey*: asphalt) / Roundabout *rotonda*
N-11	Main road [N-] *Nacional* (*red*: additional traffic and hazard)
A-1	Motorway *autopista* (*blue*: conventional motorway colour)
++++++	Railway *ferrocarril* / Station *estación*

●●●●●●	Main Waymarked route (*yellow*: ± 80% of pilgrims)
●●●●●●	Alternative Scenic route (*green*: more remote / less pilgrims)
●●●●●●	Alternative road route (*grey*: more asphalt & traffic)
●●●●●●	Optional detour *desvío* (*turquoise:* to point of interest)
●●●●●●	Primary Path of pilgrimage (*purple*: inner path of Soul)

Ⅺ ? Ɵ	Crossing *cruce* / Option *opción* / Extra care ¡cuidado!
↑ ⋇ ↑	Windmill *molino* / Viewpoint *punto de vista* / Radio mast
▪—▪/▪—▪	National boundary / Provincial boundary *límite provincial*
~/~	River *río* / Riverlet Stream *arroyo / rego*
◯/◯	Sea or lake *Mar o lago* / Woodland *bosques*
♱ ♱ †	Church *iglesia* / Chapel *capilla* / Wayside cross *cruceiro*

Ⓕ ◻ ♒	Drinking font *fuente* / Café / Shop (*mini*)*mercado*
Rst. menú V.	Restaurant / *menú peregrino* / *V. Vegetariano(a)*
ℤ 🏠 Ⅹ	Tourist office *turismo* / Manor house *pazo* / Rest area *picnic*
⊕ ⊕ ✉	Pharmacy *farmacia* / Hospital / Post office *correos*
⊕ 🚏 ⛽	Airport / Bus station *estación de autobús / gasolinera*
⁑ *XIIc.*	Ancient monument / 12th century

Ⓗ Ⓟ Ⓒ	Hotels •*H-H*****€30-90 / Pension •*P**€20+ / •*CR (B&B)* €35+
x12	Number of private rooms €35-45 (Av. single/double prices *approx*)
Ⓗ Ⓐ Ⓐ	*Off* route accommodation /Ⓐ currently closed – *check for updates*
Ⓐ❶❷	Pilgrim hostel(s) *Albergue* ● *Alb.* + Youth hostel *Juventude*
[32]	Number of bed spaces (usually bunk beds *literas*) €5-€17
[÷4] +12	÷ number of dormitories / *+12* +number of private rooms €30+

Par.	Parish hostel *Parroquial* donation / €5
Conv.	Convent or monastery hostel *donativo* / €5
Mun/Xunta	Municipal hostel €5+ / Galician government *Xunta* €8
Asoc.	Association hostel €8+
Priv. (*)	Private hostel (network*) €10-17
	(all prices average (low season) for comparison purposes only)

▭	Town plan *plan de la ciudad* with page number
(Pop.– Alt. m)	Town population – altitude in metres
▱	City suburbs / outskirts *afueras* (*grey*)
	Historical centre *centro histórico / barrio antiguo* (*brown*)

Overview: There is too much paraphernalia in our lives – in an effort to lighten the load we have produced this slim hybrid edition combining both caminos Sanabrés and Invierno which share the last few stages into Santiago. This has been made possible by the selfless work of pilgrim associations that have waymarked both routes such that, today, we need only the barest information to get us to our destination. It would be difficult to get lost if we remain present to each moment and attentive for the yellow arrows pointing the way to Santiago – mindfulness is the key. Take time to familiarise yourself with the map symbols opposite.

The standard and cost of pilgrim accommodation ranges from hostels by donation *donativo* (rare), *Xunta* hostels offering basic facilities from €8 (no prior booking) to private hostels from €10-17 but often with additional facilities such as washing machines *lavadoras* and dryers *secadora* – the latter a real boon in wet weather. The cost of hotels varies widely depending on season; many offer a pilgrim discount but ask before reserving *(discounts not generally available through websites such as www.booking.com)*. A basic 3 course meal with wine *menú peregrino* costs around €9.

The multilingual maps recognise the international fellowship of the camino. This helps foster a sense of camaraderie and communion; a shared spiritual intention that lies at the heart of pilgrimage. It is this transcendent focus that distinguishes pilgrimage from long distance walking. If you require detailed notes on preparation check the website: *www.caminoguides.com*

All of us travel two paths simultaneously; the outer path along which we haul our physical body and the inner pathway of soul. We need to be mindful of both and take time to prepare ourselves accordingly The traditional way of the pilgrim is to travel alone, by foot, carrying all the material possessions we might need for the journey. This provides the first lesson for the pilgrim – to leave behind all that is superfluous and to travel with only the barest necessities. Preparation for the inner path is similar – we start by letting go of psychic waste accumulated over the years such as resentments, prejudices and outmoded belief systems. Walking with an open mind and open heart allows us to assimilate the lessons to be found along these ancient paths of Inner Enquiry.

We have been asleep a long time. Despite the chaotic world around us, or perhaps because of it, something is stirring us to awaken from our collective amnesia. A sign of this awakening is the number of people drawn to walk the caminos. The hectic pace of modern life, experienced not only in our work but also our family and social lives, spins us ever outwards away from our centre. We have allowed ourselves to be thrown onto the surface of our lives – mistaking busyness for aliveness, but this superficial existence is inherently unsatisfying.

Pilgrimage offers us an opportunity to slow down and allow some spaciousness into our lives. In this quieter space we can reflect on the deeper significance of our lives and the reasons why we came here. The camino encourages us to ask the perennial question – Who am I? And, crucially, it provides time for answers to be understood and integrated. So let's not rush the camino but take the time it takes because it may prove a pivotal turning point in our lives. We may find that Santiago is not the end of the way but the beginning of something entirely new. Whichever route we take, our ultimate Destination is assured. The only choice we have is how long it takes us to arrive *buen camino*.

John Brierley

Covid-19 brought with it much grief and its impact on many levels will be felt for years to come. This is no less true for the camino as in any other sphere of life. Pilgrim infrastructure and albergues that took decades to put in place are struggling to survive, some have already closed and others will follow. Check the website under 'Updates' and please email *jb@caminoguides.com* with any changes you find along the way. The virus was named by the World Health Organisation as, 'An enemy against humanity'. This is an unfortunate epithet because, from Gaia's perspective, humanity itself has become the most destructive force on the planet. If the devastation that arose from this pandemic brings about a paradigm shift in human consciousness it may yet contain a blessing in disguise. For at least a generation we have, collectively, lived beyond the means of the planet to sustain us and all of life that surrounds us. We are not the only sentient beings that occupy the earth and we have wilfully and woefully ignored the plight of nature herself.

Now, today, we can change the way we think and act. We can move from fear to love. We can choose to respect each other and the natural world that is our home. We can... But will we? Each of us is part of the whole we call humankind and artificial borders can separate us no more. Indeed they never have but only in our deluded and limited understanding of the nature of reality. Coronavirus taught us that we are all part of the same delicate balance of life on earth. Will we heed its warning or revert to business as usual ... until the next crisis strikes again?

We have yet to learn the simple act of walking the earth like brothers.

Martin Luther King Jr.

The photo opposite shows a pilgrim crossing the medieval bridge *A Ponte de Taboada*. This is the point where the Winter Way merges with the Camino Sanabrés. Both, in turn, connecting with a larger network of caminos that link us with the rest of Europe and, by extension to every nation on earth. The great insight of the First Nations has always been to remind us that, *Man did not weave the web of life, he is merely a strand in it. Whatever he does to the web, he does to himself... We may yet find we are brothers after all.*

This guidebook is the latest addition to the CaminoGuides family. It has been produced in belated recognition of the ancient way from the historic city of Ourense *camino Sanabrés* and the Ribeiro Sacra valley route from Ponferrada known as *camino Invierno*. Each route offers a very different experience but both converge in the hamlet of *A Laxe* to continue as one into Santiago past the legendary *Pico Sacro* a mythical link that ties these caminos together (see stage 5) they are, accordingly, combined in one volume.

These routes also provide us with unrivalled access to one of the largest concentration of Roman artefacts and Romanesque architecture in Europe. This includes walking through the largest gold mines in the Roman Empire (World Heritage Site) and free use of the Roman Baths in Ourense! Greater use of these routes will also help answer the concern at overcrowding of the camino Francés through Sarria and Arzúa – around ¼ million in 2019. This includes pilgrims joining the route from the *camino del Norte* incl. *Viejo* (from Bilbao), *San Salvador* (Oviedo) and *Vadiniense* (San Vicente via Picos de Europa). The main Camino Norte joins the camino Francés in Arzúa.

Sarria is the most populous starting point of all routes as it provides the minimum distance (100 km) required for those hoping to receive the Compostela but with only one week to complete their journey. 88,509 pilgrims commenced their journey in the town in 2019. By contrast only 72 started in Monforte de Lemos on the camino Invierno which also qualifies for a Compostela being over the requisite 100 km rule. Numbers for the Camino Sanabrés are more difficult to assess as pilgrims commencing their journey along the Via de la Plata have an option in Granja de Moreruela to keep straight on north to join the camino Francés in Astorga or to branch off west along the Camino Sanabrés via Ourense. What we do know is that only 365 commenced their pilgrimage in Puebla de Sanabria, the official starting point for the camino Sanabrés, after which it is named, and 3,763 started in Ourense.

Ourense offers a much more accessible starting point than Sarria as the latter is reached by a very limited and indirect bus service via Lugo. Conversely Ourense has a daily schedule of up to 20 regular bus and rail services direct from Santiago taking an average of 90 minutes. This is augmented by daily direct services from several cities including direct services from Madrid airport for those travelling from outside Spain. It defies logic as to why Ourense has not been more widely used. Over many years it has developed good facilities and lodging at reasonable distances and prices. It is thus a perfect first camino in its own right or ideal for those who have to fit their camino into one week. Facilities are likely to be tested in the years ahead with the anticipated uplift in pilgrim numbers but the overall infrastructure is good with excellent road and public transport if needed. Much of it is on earthen paths mostly through ancient oak woods offering shade from sun or the more ubiquitous rain or wind.

The Oaknut *Quercus* a fitting symbol for the Ourense route although we have colour-coded the route *silver* in recognition that it is part of the camino Sanabrés which is, in turn, a branch of the Via de la Plata which is more frequently identified as the silver *plata* route. But this serves our purpose well as it differentiates the camino Invierno which we have colour-coded gold *oro* in recognition of that the fact it goes

directly through the Roman gold mines of Las Médulas. Both routes are now well waymarked.

Ponferrada is the start point for the Winter Route *Camino Invierno* providing a partial solution to the overcrowding of the route through Sarria. Here we are offered a stunning alternative route to Santiago. It is 158 km longer (275-v-117 km) requiring an additional 6 stages (10-v-4 km). It is ideal for anyone who has previously walked the camino Francés and would like to avoid the bustle of the camino from Sarria and explore a quieter and more challenging finale to their camino. It offers the pioneering spirit and experience of those who set out on the camino Francés in the 1970's or the camino Portugués the following decade. On this account it suits the seasoned pilgrim able to go the 'extra mile' to find a place to eat or sleep. Conversely it is currently *not* ideal for those setting out for their first camino. While waymarking is now good, lodging is haphazard and spaced at inconvenient stages which requires careful prior planning. Much of the limited lodging was developed for tourism which increases prices particularly on the first stage around Las Médulas. But new pilgrim hostels are opening and there are plans to increase these in key locations, but this will take time.

The Chestnut is a fitting symbol for the camino Invierno as the Romans expanded its use as a way to feed the gold-miners along the río Sil as the land was poor and not capable of producing wheat or other crops as a staple diet. There is a small interpretive centre *Aula del Castaños* in Borrenes (stage 01) which sets out the importance of the chestnut harvest since Roman times and which is still ongoing to this day. The chestnut is

found everywhere along the camino especially in the Las Médulas area and Ourense remains one of the main chestnut exporters in the world.

Ribeira Sacra In the meantime we can explore one of the most beautiful and undiscovered caminos that runs along the majestic río Sil with its extensive vineyards *viñedos* interspersed by the ubiquitous chestnut *castaños*. In 1996 Ribeira Sacra was designated DO *Denominación de Origen* for its fine wines grown along the banks of the rios Sil and Miño. The vineyards are planted on steep and narrow terraces *bancadas* producing a grape of a singular and concentrated flavour. The three best known classic grape varieties from the area are the exquisite and ubiquitous red **Mencía** (photo above) and two exceptional whites **Albariño & Godello**. The etymology of Ribeira Sacra is instructive. Originally from Latin for Sacred Oak Grove *Roboira Sacrata* a mistranslation by a monk in the eighteenth century changed it to Sacred Riverside *Ribeira Sacra!* Either translation fits the description well. Wine production was an obvious choice for the steep sided river valleys and the micro-climate was conducive to their growth. The vineyards were subsequently taken over by the numerous monasteries and hermitages that sprang up along the relatively inaccessible river valleys in the Middle Ages. There is an excellent wine museum and interpretive centre in Monforte de Lemos (stage 05).

Galicia: Historical Snapshot, Brief Chronology and Mythology:

What follows is not a scholarly or historical treatise. It is included as a context in which to understand better the land we journey through and a reason why we are here. It appears on a yellow panel so you can easily skip this section if you have read it in one of the other guidebooks or if it is of no interest. It merely seeks to draw together some of the innumerable strands that make the camino routes through Galicia so enduring and which have drawn pilgrims from every single nation on earth to explore the unique part we each play in the awakening of humankind and the urgent need for a paradigm shift in our collective consciousness.

While Finisterre may lie at the heart of the Santiago story each route makes its own unique contribution and this is no less valid for the caminos that are described in this guide and that commence in Ourense or Ponferrada. As noted elsewhere, belief and legend should not be confused with the truth to which they point. We may miss the point entirely if we only take the literal view and try and drag the mystical into the factual. The boundary between the metaphysical and physical worlds is nowhere thinner than along the caminos that thread their way through Galicia. Let's not miss the opportunity to step over the threshold into the experience of our True Nature.

Onwards & upwards! *¡ultreia et suseia!...*

• *Megalithic period c. 4000 B.C.E*

History tells us little about the Neolithic peoples who inhabited the western fringes of Europe. However, evidence of their stonework can be found all over the Galician landscape and goes back at least 6,000 years as seen in the petroglyphs and rock art of 4,000 B.C.E and the dolmens *mamoas* of the same period. These mega-monuments are dotted all around Galicia. This megalithic culture was deeply religious in nature and left a powerful impact on the peoples who followed.

• *Early Celtic period c. 1000 B.C.E*

Central European Celts settled in western Spain inter-marrying with the Iberians. These Celti-Iberians were the forebears of the Celtic Nerios peoples who came to inhabit Galicia centuries before the Roman occupation. Remains of their Celtic villages *castros* can still be seen around the remote countryside. These fortified villages were built in a circular formation usually occupying some elevated ground or hillock. The extensive mineral deposits of Galicia gave rise to a rich artistic movement and Celtic bronze and gold artefacts from this area can be seen in museums all across Europe.

Galicia remains one of the least well known of the Celtic nations and yet it is one of the oldest. Galician Celts trace their mythic lineage to the king of Scythia in the Black sea area where the Druid Caichar had a vision in which he saw them travelling west to found Galicia and Ireland. The first Gaelic colony was established in Galicia under Brath and his son Breogán the latter becoming the legendary hero who founded Brigantium (present day A Coruña) entering folklore and the national anthem of Galicia in the process, '*Wake up from your dreams, home of Breogán.*' His grandson became King Milesius after whom the Celtic Milesians were named. It is generally accepted that the first Celts to settle in Ireland were Milesians from Galicia. In a masterful stroke of genius early Christian monks then extended the Celtic lineage 36 generations back to link it with the biblical Adam!

• *Early Christian Period c. 40 C.E.*

While there is no historical evidence to support the view that St. James preached in Galicia, there are some anecdotal references to that effect. (*see photo of Santiago Peregrino from the parish church in Finisterre. This church also has a statue of Christ much revered in Galicia and associated with many miracles*). It would appear that St. James sailed to Galicia, probably Padrón, to preach Christ's message, his body being brought back there after his martyrdom in Jerusalem around 40

C.E It is reasonable to assume that he, or his followers, would have sought to bring the Christian message to areas of spiritual significance on which to graft its own message. Finisterre was one of the most significant spiritual sites in the world at that time and it was inevitable that it would draw those with a spiritual mission. It was also accessible, being directly on the sea route from Palestine. However, sea routes were not the only ways to access this corner of the world and Roman roads were being built that linked Portugal and Spain to France and the rest of Europe.

• *Early Roman period 100 B.C.E*

By the end of the first century the Romans controlled most of the southern Iberian peninsular naming the unruly northern province *Hispania Ulterior* to include the area known as *Gallaecia*. In 61 BC Julius Caesar became governor and conducted naval expeditions along the coast and finally wrested control of the Atlantic seaboard from the Phoenicians. In 136 the proconsul Decimus Junius Brutus led his legions across the Lima and Minho rivers to enter Gallaecia for the first time. He met resistance not only from the fierce inhabitants but also from his own soldiers wary of crossing the river *Lima* thought to represent one of the rivers of Hades – the river of forgetfulness *Lethe*. Brutus became the first Roman general to make it to Finisterre 'by road' and was reputedly mesmerised at the way the sea 'drank up' the sun and was

predisposed to the pagan and Druidic worship centred on the Phoenician Altar to the Sun *Ara Solis*. The Romans perseverance in conquering this corner of Hispania was, however, more prosaic being primarily due to its rich mining potential. A Roman milestone *miliario romano* from the first century *Via XVIII Romano* is located in A Rua stage 03 of camino Invierno *(see photo>)*.

Gold was found in small quantities in Galicia long before the Romans turned production along the Sil valley into the largest goldmines in the Empire mining upwards of a hundred tons during their occupation (see under Las Médulas). Ourense was founded by the Romans who also unearthed the largest body of geothermal waters in Europe. These hot springs *Termas* or *Burgas* were a major part of Roman life (the Roman baths are still extant and can be enjoyed today). Ourense was also one of the easiest ways to cross the Miño River and so it became a city of strategic importance. (We cross the Roman bridge *Ponte Vella* on our first stage of the camino Sanabrés (see under Ourense).

• *The Middle Ages 476 – 1453*

Hispania was the Latin name given to the whole Iberian peninsula. After the fall of the Roman Empire in 476 C.E. the north-western province (present

day Galicia) was ruled by the Vandals, Suevi and Visigoths, descendants of the Germanic tribes that had overrun Roman Hispania leading to its collapse. It is hard to believe (and little understood) that the Moorish 'invasion' of the Iberian peninsula in 711 was actually an invitation to the forces of Islam by the squabbling Visigoth nobles to help in their domestic feuds.

The Umayyad Muslims were happy to oblige and so the invasion by invitation began. Muslim forces quickly moved north to conquer the whole peninsular, capturing the bells of Santiago cathedral along the way and infamously taking them to Granada. But Galicia proved impossible to control and Islamic rule here lasted only a few decades. It was to take another 700 years before the re-conquest was complete in the south – and the bells returned to Santiago. But they left behind some exquisite art and architecture most notably in the iconic Mozarabic arch with its horseshoe shape *(see photo above of the interior of Iglesia de Santo Tomás in Ponferrada).*

Even the briefest sketch of Spanish history would not be complete without looking at the contribution of the Templar knights both to the reconquest *reconquista* of the Iberian peninsular from Islamic rule to Christianity but also its subsequent support of the pilgrimage routes to (and from) Santiago. These warrior monks originated in Jerusalem in 1118 B.C.E. with a vow to 'protect pilgrims on the roads leading to Jerusalem'. Their headquarters were located in part of the original Solomon's Temple or Temple Mount. After

the Holy Land was 'lost' to Islam the whole centre of focus was switched to the reconquest of Spain. This is when the image of St. James the Moor-slayer *Santiago Matamoros* first appeared on a white charger to spearhead the *reconquista*. Behind this powerful and terrifying image of St. James with the slain moors at his feet (see photo) came the Knights Templar mounted on their own chargers and dressed in their familiar white tunics emblazoned with the Templar Cross.

Once the reconquest was complete the Knights switched their role to protecting the pilgrim from other perils of the road. In 1307 the French monarch Philippe IV moved against the Knights in an attempt to purloin their considerable fortunes to alleviate his own financial problems and the Order 'blended' into the Hospitallers. The Camino Invierno encompasses two of the most prominent Templar castles in Spain at Ponferrada and Cornatel. Both have been well preserved and well deserving of a visit.

• *The Catholic Monarchs 1469 – 1516*

The marriage in 1469 of Isabella I of Castille and Fernando II of Aragón saw the merging of two of the most powerful kingdoms in Spain. The title Catholic Monarchs *los Reyes Católicos* was bestowed by Pope Alexander VI with an eye to aiding the re-conquest and unifying Spain under Roman Catholicism. This was finally achieved after the conquest of the Muslim Kingdom of Granada in 1492, the same year Columbus 'discovered' the Americas. This illustrious period was tarnished by the expulsion or massacre of non-Catholics under the infamous Inquisition initiated under her reign. Isabella is, perhaps, best remembered for her more beneficent activities such as the building of the pilgrim hospital in Santiago, now the luxurious *parador Hostal Dos Reis Católicos* – reputedly the oldest hotel in the world in continuous occupation for that purpose.

• *The War(s) of Independence 1807 – 1814*

Despite its remote location, Galicia was not spared the effects of the War of Independence 'Peninsular War' (1807–1814) when forces of Napoleon ransacked many of the villages along which we pass through. The Peninsular was a military conflict between Napoleon's empire and Bourbon Spain for control of the Iberian Peninsula during the Napoleonic Wars. It began when the French and Spanish invaded Portugal in 1807 and escalated the following year when France turned on its former ally Spain and lasted until Napoleon was defeated in 1814. The Peninsular War overlaps with the Spanish War of Independence *Guerra de la Independencia Española* which began with the uprising on 2 May 1808 *Dos de Mayo (still remembered in many a street name)*.

• *The Carlist Wars & First Spanish Republic 1833 – 1876*

The Carlist Wars followed between followers of Carlos V and his descendants fighting for absolutist Monarch supported by the Catholic church against the forces of liberalism and republicanism. Towards the end of the 3rd Carlist war the first Spanish Republic was proclaimed in 1873. Again the remoteness of Galicia was no bar to its involvement in anti-monarchist activities. Indeed its resistance to any outside interference continues to this day.

No introduction to Galicia would be complete without mention of Castelao who was born in Rianxo in 1886 and who died in Buenos Aires in 1950. Politician, writer, and doctor. Identified as a founding father of Galician nationalism, identity and culture and president of the Galician Gelegust Party. He presented the idea of an independent Galician State *Estatuto de Galicia* to the Spanish Parliament in the same year that General Franco appeared on the political scene. Despite various initiatives to earn independence for Galicia it was not until 1981 that it achieved a measure of autonomy, being recognised as a separate autonomous region in that year. A footnote to his life suggests that he was a convinced pro-European. He wrote in *Sempre en Galiza* that one of his dreams was to, 'see the emergence of a United States of Europe'.

● *The Spanish Civil War 1936 –1939 & Franco Period.*

In 1936 General Franco seized power leading to one of the bloodiest civil wars in history and its effects can still be felt today despite the 'Pact of Forgetting' *Pacto del Olvido*. This was a decision by all parties to the conflict to avoid dealing with the horrifying legacy of Fascism under Franco. The Pact attempted to transition from an autocratic to democratic rule of law without recriminations for the countless thousands killed summarily and buried in unmarked graves throughout Spain. While suppression of painful memories helped in national reconciliation at that time – these memories remain close to the surface. There is a growing body of opinion within Spain today that it should now take a more honest and open look at the violence of that period.

The Spanish Civil War *Guerra Civil Española* pitted Republicans (with Communist and Socialist sympathies), against the Nationalists a predominantly conservative Catholic and Fascist grouping led by General Francisco Franco. Fascism prevailed not least owing to the intervention of Nazi Germany and Fascist Italy who provided weapons, soldiers and air bombardment (Guernica). This struggle between democracy and fascism for the soul of Spain was to last until Franco's death in 1975.

● *Galicia Today 1975 – 2020*

After Franco's death King Carlos nominally succeeded and appointed political reformist Adolfo Suárez to form a government. In 1982 the Spanish Socialist Workers' Party *Partido Socialista Obrero Español* **PSOE** won a sweeping victory under Felipe González who successfully steered Spain into full membership of the EEC in 1986, In 1996 José María Aznar, leader of the centre-right People's Party *Partido Popular* **PP** won a narrow mandate but in 2002 the oil tanker Prestige ran into a storm off Finisterre and the ensuing ecological catastrophe sank not only the livelihood of scores of Galician fisherman but, in due time, the right wing government as well resulting in a popular cry up and down the country of 'never again' *nunca maís*.

It only took the government's unpopular support of the invasion of Iraq linked to the Madrid bombings in March 2004 to put the socialist's back in power under the youthful leadership of José Luis Rodríguez Zapatero. The new government set in motion an immediate change in foreign policy and, more controversially, a sudden but decisive shift from a conservative Catholic to a liberal secular society that led to one newspaper headline, *'Church and State square up in struggle for the spirit of Spain.'* The State, propped up with its banking and commercial sectors, appears to have won the day. But the deep-seated spirituality of Spain lies not far below the surface and the resurgence of the caminos is one sign that it is alive and making a comeback.

The Banking collapse of 2008 and the deepening economic crisis led to the re-election of the conservative **PP** in December 2011 under Mariano Rajoy. However, in 2018 the **PP** was again ousted due to corruption scandals & socialist Pedro Sanchez formed a new socialist alliance in 2019 between **PSOE** *(28%)* Pablo Iglesias of United We Can *Unidas Podemos* **UP** *(12%)* in part to keep the emerging far-right party **VOX** *(15%)* from forming an alliance with the **PP** *(20%)*. Do the maths and you will see it is close run thing and we can expect more upheaval before too long! ...and seemingly oblivious to all these social and political upheavals, the *caminos* go quietly about their gentle spirit of positive transformation.

Galician Culture: The flowering of Galician art that took place under Alfonso VII and Ferdinand II (kings of Galicia until it was absorbed into León and Castille under Ferdinand III) saw the completion of the great cathedrals of Ourense, Lugo and Tui, as well as Santiago. However, between the three great powers comprising the Catholic monarchy, the Aristocracy and Castille; Galician art, culture and language were greatly diluted. Indeed while the French Way *Camino Francés* introduced wonderfully inspiring European art and artisans to towns all along the route to Santiago, it had the effect of diminishing the Celtic influences within Galicia.

Galician Language: The distinctive language of Galicia *Gallego* is still widely used today. The language institute estimates that 94% of the population understand it, while 88% can speak it. Gallego belongs to the Iberian Romance group of languages with some common aspects with Portuguese. Phrase books between Spanish *Castellano* Galician *Galego* and English are difficult to find but one of the more obvious differences is the substitution of the Spanish J – hard as in Junta (pron: **kh**unta) as opposed to the softer Galego Xunta (pron: **sh**unta). Here are a few common phrases to help distinguish one from the other:

The Jacobean Way	Del Camino Jacobeo	Do Camiño Xacobeo
Pilgrimage to Santiago	Peregrinaje a Santiago	Peregrinaxe a Santiago
Fountains of Galicia	Las Fuentes de Galicia	Das Fontes de Galiza
The Botanical garden	El Jardin Botanico	O Xardín Botánico
Collegiate church	Colegiata Iglesia	Colexiata Igrexa
Town Hall	Casa Consistorial	Concello da Vila
Below the main Square	Bajo el plaza mayor	Debaixo do praza maior

The Revival *Rexurdimento* of Galician language and literature in the 19th century was spearheaded with the publication in 1863 of *Cantares Gallegos* by the incomparable Galician poetess, Rosalía Castro. The Revival reached its zenith in the 1880's with the publication of many illuminating Galician texts such as *Follas Novas* also by Rosalía Castro, *Saudades Galegas* by Lamas de Carvajal and *Queixumes dos Pinos* by Eduardo Pondal. Galicia's culture has been kept alive as much by its exiles, political and economic, as by those that remained behind. The anthem of Galicia, The Pines *Os Pinos* was written and first sung in Cuba, where it urged the Galician to awaken from the yoke of servitude into freedom: *'Listen to the voices of the murmuring pines which is none other than the voices of the Galician people.'* However, even the pine trees seem under threat from the imported eucalyptus that has taken over large swathes of the countryside.

The fruits of this revival can be tasted, nonetheless, throughout Galicia today. You may well hear the swirl of the traditional Galician bagpipes *Gaita* in the bars and squares of the towns we pass through or at one of the many festivals and fairs that take place throughout the year. Many of these are based on the ancient Celtic celebration of the seasons particularly at the equinoxes and the summer and winter solstices. The short pilgrimages to local shrines *romerías* endorse the deeply held religious values of the people of Galicia but drawing ever larger crowds are the secular festivals such as the Night of the Templars *Noche Templaria* which is, in fact, a 5 day celebration of traditional markets, parades, music events and fireworks during the first week of July in Ponferrada.

Galician Nationalism appears to be born more out of a deep pride in its traditions, rather than a need to overthrow a culture that has been imposed from outside. This is not unlike other Celtic cultures that have found themselves marginalised on the Western fringes of Europe. We demean Galicia and ourselves by stereotyping popular Spanish culture onto her. This is not the Spain of castanets, paella and Rioja wines. Her identity is clearly Celtic with *gaitas, mariscos* and *Albariño* wines predominating – all of which are a cause of justified pride.

Preparation – A Quick Guide:

[1] Practical Considerations:

• **When?** Spring is often wet and windy but the routes are relatively quiet with early flowers appearing. Summer is busy and hot and hostels often full. Autumn usually provides the most stable weather with harvesting adding to the colour and celebrations of the countryside. Winter is solitary and cold with reduced daylight hours for walking and some hostels will be closed.

• **How long?** Ourense to Santiago is 108.2 km and comprises the last 5 stages of the camino Sanabrés (average daily walk of 21.6 km). Ponferrada to Santiago is 274.3 km and divided, in this guide, into 10 stages (average daily walk of 27.4 km). Interim lodging allows each stage to be varied according to differing abilities, pace and intentions.

[2] Preparation – Outer: What do I need to take

• Buy your boots in time to walk them in before you go.
• Pack a Poncho – Galicia is notorious for its downpours.
• Bring a hat – sunstroke is painful and can be dangerous.
• Look again if your backpack weighs more than 10 kilos.

If this is your first pilgrimage source more comprehensive notes on preparation at _www.caminoguides.com_

... *and* consider leaving behind.

• Books, except this one – all the maps and promptings you need are included.
• Extras, Galicia has shops if you need to replace something.
• Everything that is superfluous for pilgrimage. Take time to reflect carefully on this point as it can form the basis of our questioning of what is really important in our life and spiritual awakening. We have become reliant, even addicted, to so many extraneous 'things'. We need to de-clutter in order to clear space for what truly matters to arise in our awareness.

[3] Language: learn at least some basic phrases now, *before* you go.

[4] Pilgrim Passport: Get a *credencial* from your local confraternity – and join it (see page 22).

[5] Protocol: Have consideration for the needs of your fellow pilgrims, gratitude for your hosts and take care of nature and the Landscape Temple.

[6] Prayer: May my every step be a prayer for peace and loving kindness.

[7] Preparation *Inner*: Why is my real purpose for walking the camino?

Some Statistics: While we can never know the actual number of pilgrims who arrive into Santiago each year we do know from records kept at the Pilgrim Office *www.oficinadelperegrino.com* that a total 347,578 pilgrims collected a Compostela in 2019. Of these 40% gave a religious reason for their journey while 60% gave a spiritual or 'other' reasons for doing so. Contrary to popular belief the majority (54%) were between the ages of 30 and 60 and while there is a good gender balance women now outnumber men for the first time (51%). 94% arrived on foot, 5% arrived by bicycle, with the remaining: 406 by horseback, 243 by boat and 85 by wheelchair.

175 nations were represented last year, the majority: ❶ Spanish: 146,350 (42%) ❷ Italian 28,749 (8%) ❸ German 26,167 (7%) ❹ USA (20,652 (6%) ❺ Portugal 17,450 (5%) ❻ France 9,248 (2.7%) ❼ UK 9,132 (2.6%) ❽ Korea 8,224 (2.3%) ❾ Ireland 6,826 (2.0%) ❿ Brasil 6,025 (1.7%) ⓫ Australia 5,301 (1.5%) ⓬ Canada 5,279 (1.5%).

Pilgrims per month per camino

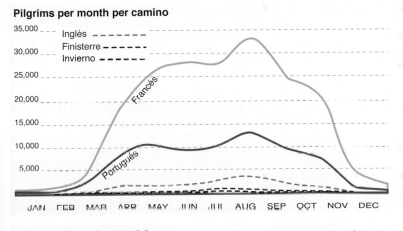

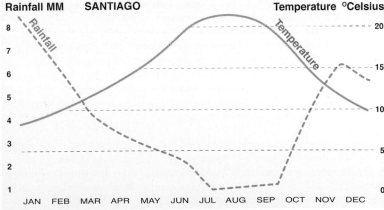

Map Legend: Once you are familiar with the map symbols (Page 4) you should be able to easily find your way and identify places to stop and eat or sleep. Unlike conventional maps you always follow in the direction of the page so that everything appears sequentially on your left or right (similar to GPS systems such as Tom Tom). **Maps** show relevant information only and are therefore not strictly to scale – instead accurate distances are given between each facility or point of interest and corresponds to the text for ease of reference. The maps are one-directional only so if you intend to walk 'in reverse' (e.g. from Santiago *to* Ourense) source a conventional map to use alongside. **Contour guides** are also shown for each day's walk. This will give you an impression of the day's terrain and help you prepare for the uphill stretches and anticipate the downhill ones. Contours are drawn to an exaggerated scale for emphasis.

Adjusted distance: In addition to *actual* distance an adjusted equivalent is also provided based on the cumulative height climbed during each stage. This equates to the additional effort and time necessary to walk the stage over and above that required if it were a purely level walk. It is based on the internationally accepted Naismith's rule. e.g. Stage 2 appears an easy **15.2** km but it has a cumulative ascent of 980m or an extra 4.9 km of effort giving an equivalent of **20.1** km for that stage! Remember also that a normal walking pace (average is 1 km in 20 minutes or 3 kph) will decrease, often substantially, towards the end of a hard day's walk. That is why pilgrims sometimes question the measurements given for the *last* section suggesting it was *double* the distance indicated (it took twice as long as expected). They were right about the time but not the distance! Take heed of the Chinese proverb, *'On a journey of a hundred miles, ninety is but half way'*!

Stages *etapas:* Each day's stage is measured from the front door of one albergue to the next. Intermediate hotels or hostels are also shown, those directly on the route in a solid panel and those *off* route with a border only (with distance).This way you can choose where to stay each night depending on your particular needs. ***Interim lodging*** is often less frequented, but generally has less bed-spaces and facilities in the more remote villages, but may well suit those requiring a more contemplative journey.

Text and place names are shown as they appear 'on the ground' which is generally in Galician *Galego* but sometimes appear in Spanish *Castellano*. The Church of St. John may, therefore, appear as *Igrexa San Xoán* or *Igreja San Juan*. Villages in Galicia, tend to straggle without any defined centre and even the local church is frequently located outside the actual town. Distances are measured to a clearly defined feature.

Abbreviations: s/o = straight on / > turn right / < left / (right) on the right / c. = circa (about) / XIIc. = 12th century / adj. = adjacent or adjoining / incl. = inclusive / imm. = immediately / para. = parallel / €pp (per person). c/ = calle (street). r/ = rúa (road) / Av. = avenida (avenue) / ●*Alb.* = albergue (pilgrim hostal) / •*Apt.* = apartment / •*Hs* = hostal / €25-40 (single–double).

Safety: The camino offers a remarkably safe environment in an inherently unsafe world. When viewed in this context few cases of crime or harassment are reported but they have been known to occur. If you are a solo pilgrim and feel unsafe, keep other pilgrims in sight or ask to walk with someone until you feel comfortable again. Tim Cahill suggests, *'A journey is best measured in friends, rather than miles'*. In the event of an emergency or to report an incident the EU wide emergency number is 112. Road traffic is the major safety concern and extra vigilance is needed while on or crossing roadways.

Mobile Phones: One of the more obvious changes along the camino is the exponential rise in mobile phones and their impact on our individual and collective experience. The constant connectivity with our familiar *outer* world can keep us disconnected from the expansiveness of our *inner* world. This disconnect is multi-layered. It can diminish our relationship to each passing moment, the camaraderie of our 'camino family' and connection to our divine essence. Finding the courage to step outside our comfort zone can lead to Self-discovery. This may require limiting our dependency on external aids. While many of us may feel the need to carry a mobile phone for safety, orientation or other reasons perhaps we can, collectively, be more conscious about how and when we use them so as to minimise disturbance to other pilgrims... and ourSelves. See: *www.walkingtopresence.com*

Sun Compass: this is provided on each map as an aid to orientation. Even in poor weather we can generally tell the direction of the sun. The general direction of these routes is westerly. Early in the morning the sun will be in the east and therefore 'behind' us and will gradually move around to appear over our left shoulder at midday. If you suddenly find yourself walking with the sun over your right shoulder – stop and make sure you are not following arrows *back* to your start point! In the evening the sun will be in our face so, likewise, if the sun is behind you – stop and re-assess. You can 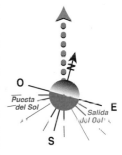 also use this compass as an aid to understanding the human egoic tendency to identify ourselves as being at the centre of the universe. We say that the sun rises in the east *este* because that is our experience but of course it is the earth turning on its axis that turns us towards the sun in the morning and away from it at night.

This is more than mere semantics – the very thought used to be a heresy punishable by death as Galileo was also to discover. To understand why Finisterre is at the centre of the Santiago story we need to realise the vital importance of the sun and its orientation to ancient civilisations – not only its veneration as the source of life and regeneration with the rising sun *salida del sol* but its symbol of death and resurrection through the setting sun *puesta del sol* in the West *Oeste*.

Pilgrim Passport *Credencial***:** All official pilgrim hostels are reserved exclusively for pilgrims on the camino who must have a pilgrim passport *credencial* that has been stamped along the way. To apply for a **Compostela** you need to have your credencial stamped twice daily over the last 100km (from Ourense or Chantada on the camino Invierno). This second stamp requirement was recently introduced in an effort to eliminate those using interim transport or whose main intention was to collect a certificate rather than *bona fide*

pilgrims embarking on a spiritual journey. Stamps *sellos* are readily available from churches, hostels, hotels, even bars. These passports are available from your local confraternity and you are encouraged to join and support the largely voluntary work of these organisations (see list of addresses at the back).

Apply for your credencial in good time although some pilgrim associations now provide an internet application which speeds processing. If you have been unable to acquire a credencial before travelling – don't worry as these are widely available in Ourense or Ponferrada and along the route.

Pilgrim hostels *albergues de peregrinos* vary in what they provide but lodging is usually in bunk beds with additional overflow space on mattresses *colchonetas*. Number of beds is shown [in brackets] and also number of dormitories (simple division will provide an idea of density!). All Xunta and municipal hostels provide a kitchen with basic cooking equipment and a dining / sitting area. Opening times vary depending on the time of year but are generally cleaned and open again from early afternoon (14:00) to welcome pilgrims. You cannot reserve a bed in advance and phone numbers are provided for emergency calls or to check availability outside the normal seasons (most are open all year but can close for holidays or maintenance purposes). *Note: Albergues are likely to come under new tourist regulations requiring additional facilities. If enforced this may raise the price of accommodation significantly.*

Costs: Some monastery *convento Conv.* & parish *paroquia Par.* hostals ask for donations *donativo* and, unless we find ourselves destitute, we should leave at least €5 for a bed + €2 for basic breakfast and €8 for supper. Municipal hostals *Mun.* start at €6, Xunta *Xun.* €8 and Private hostels *Priv.* €10-€17. This generally provides us with a bunk bed and use of a hot shower. Many offer additional facilities such as use of washing and drying machines for a small charge and many private hostals also provide individual rooms from around €25+. Hotels *H*, hostales *Hs*, pensiónes *P* or casa rurales *CR* literally 'rural house' (a type of up-market B&B) vary widely from €30-€90 depending on season and facilities offered. Where a price range is shown in this guide the lower price is based on one person per night *individual* and the higher for 2 people sharing *doble*. Allow for a basic *minimum* €25 a day to include overnight stay at a Xunta hostel and remainder for food and drink. Some hostals provide a communal dinner (dependent on the warden *hospitalero*) and most have a basic kitchen *cocina* where a meal can be prepared. Alternatively most locations have one or more restaurants to choose from. Pilgrim menus *menú peregrino* are generally available for around €9 incl. wine. If you want to indulge in the wonderful seafood *mariscos* available in Galicia and accompany this with the delightful local *Albariño* wines expect to double or treble the basic cost!

Travel to OURENSE: *(check www.rome2rio.com)*

From Santiago: Train – every half hour during the day with journey time of 40 minutes and cost around €20 *renfe.com* **Bus** every hour during the day with journey time of 1 hour 45 minutes and cost around €10 *monbus.es (N.B. alight at bus stop on Av. Santiago close to Ponte Romano the pedestrian entrance into the city. Do NOT go to the main bus station which is 1.5 km further out of town)*. **Taxi** – takes around 1 hour €150. From **Madrid** – Bus direct 3 times a day 6 ½ hours €50 *www.avanzabus.com* / *www.alsa.com/en*

Travel to PONFERRADA: *(check www.rome2rio.com)*

From Santiago: Train – every hour during the day with journey time of 2 hours 50 minutes cost around €25 *www.renfe.com/es/en* **Bus** every 4 hours during the day with journey time of 3 hour 40 minutes (via A Coruña and Lugo) cost around €30 *www.alsa.com/en* From **Madrid** – Bus direct (from airport) 4 times a day 5 hours €35 *www.alsa.com/en*

Returning: When planning your return note that Galicia has 3 airports: Santiago, A Coruña and Vigo. Also there are regular and fast bus and rail services direct to Porto Airport *www.alsa.com/en* with journey time around 4 hours (via Vigo and Tui) cost ±€25.

How you arrive at your point of departure and whichever route you take do take time to prepare a purpose for this pilgrimage and complete the self-assessment questionnaire on the next page. We might benefit by starting from the premise that we are essentially spiritual beings on a human journey, not human beings on a spiritual one. We came to learn an essential lesson and pilgrimage affords an opportunity to find out what that is. Ask for help and expect it – it's there, now, waiting for us...

SELF-ASSESSMENT *INNER WAYMARKS*

This self-assessment questionnaire is designed to encourage us to reflect on our life and its direction. We might view it as a snapshot of this moment in our evolving life-story. In the busyness that surrounds us we often fail to take stock of where we are headed. We are the authors of our unfolding drama and can re-write the script anytime we choose. Our next steps are up to us...

We might find it useful to initially answer these questions in quick succession as this may allow a more intuitive response. Afterwards, we can reflect more deeply and check if our intellectual response confirms these, change them or bring in other insights. Download copies of the questionnaire from the *Camino Guides* website – make extra copies so you can repeat the exercise on your return and again in (say) 6 months time. This way we can compare results and ensure we follow through on any insights and commitments that come to us while walking the camino.

❐ How do I differentiate pilgrimage from a long distance walk?
❐ How do I define spirituality – what does it mean to me?
❐ How is my spirituality expressed at home and at work?

❐ What do I see as the primary purpose of my life?
❐ Am I working consciously towards fulfilling that purpose?
❐ How clear am I on my goal and the right direction for me at this time?
❐ How will I recognise resistance to any changes required to reach my goal?

❐ When did I first become aware of a desire to take time-out?
❐ What prompted me originally to go on the camino de Santiago?
❐ Did the prompt come from something that I felt needed changing?
❐ Make a list of what appears to be blocking any change from happening.

❐ What help might I need on a practical, emotional and spiritual level?
❐ How will I recognise the right help or correct answer?
❐ What are the likely challenges in working towards my unique potential?
❐ What are my next steps towards fulfilling that potential?

How aware am I of the following? (score on a level of 1 – 10)
Compare these scores again on returning from the camino.

❐ Awareness of my inner spiritual world
❐ Clarity on what inspires me and the capacity to live my passion
❐ Confidence to follow my intuitive sense of the 'right' direction
❐ Ability to recognise the false egoic guide and the 'wrong' direction
❐ Ability to recognise my resistances and patterns of defence
❐ Ease with asking for, and receiving, support from others

REFLECTIONS:

"I am doing the camino once again, looking for something I left behind or perhaps never found. It's like coming home." Notes of a pilgrim from New Mexico. What are *my* reflections for this day?

_____

_____

_____

_____

_____

_____

_____

_____

_____

_____

_____

_____

_____

_____

_____

_____

_____

_____

_____

_____

_____

_____

Going deeper? View www.inner-camino.com for guidance along the inner path.

Ponte Romano — Ourense

A PILGRIM'S GUIDE TO THE

Camino Sanabrés
Ourense – A Laxe – Santiago

Ano Santo do Xacobeo MMXXI
Inaugural Edition for the Holy Year of St. James 2021

*A Practical & Mystical Manual
for the Modern-day Pilgrim*

John Brierley

■ **Background:** Ourense (Galician: *Orense*) is a thriving modern city which combines a rich Roman heritage with the more traditional elements of Galician culture and a vibrant student life. It was an important stop on the Via de Plata in the medieval period and there are many artefacts and reminders of St. James in the city today.

Ourense cathedral **Catedral de San Martiño XII-XIIIc.** (founded in 570) occupies the heart of the historic old town *casco viejo*. Romanesque in style (later additions) it sits under a magnificent Gothic dome. It has many Compostelan motifs most notably the 'Door of Glory' *Portico de la Gloria* modelled on the cathedral in Santiago on its western facade. There are several entrances into the cathedral from the surrounding streets but it is impossible to get any sense of the enormity of the building because it is 'hidden' behind other edifices. The best place to get a view of the whole complex is from the **Mirador de San Francisco** (steep steps up Rua Estrella). The interior is particularly rich in Jacobean symbols with an unusual and delightful 18th century image of the Virgin Pilgrim **Virxe Peregrina** *(see photo above)*. The gold clad Christ's Chapel **Capilla del Cristo XVIc.** contains a crucifix venerated throughout Galicia and reminiscent of the Christ with the Golden Beard *Cristo da Barba Dourada* in the church of Santa Maria in Finisterre.

Ourense *(arriving by rail or bus see page 23)* third largest city in Galicia with a population of 110,000. It is the capital of the province which has seen dramatic growth in the past 2 decades from 307,000 to 430,000. It owes much of its significance to the Romans who were attracted by the hot springs known as **As Burgas**. This attracts the modern tourist too and Ourense is home to the largest geothermal springs in Europe (3 million litres per day!) Temperatures range from 36° – 72° degrees Celsius. We can avail of several of these hot springs *pozas*, mostly on the northern bank of the Miño river beyond the millennium bridge *Ponte do Milenio (see photo below)*.

One of the more popular hot springs *A Chavasqueira* with public and private baths in small outdoor natural pools varying in temperature. Known as the Bishop's hot springs *Caldas do Bispo (Bishop Quevedo commissioned them for patients seeking thermal cures)*. The private baths are subject to availability, or pre-book, with small entrance fee that includes locker, showers and swim hat and towels are available. However, one of the most accessible is located in the old town adjacent to the pilgrim hostel. It is free of charge and a wonderful place to relax muscles, if not the mind, as it follows the ancient Roman usage as a sociable place to catch up on current affairs... and where to find the best restaurants! Ourense is not only home to these hot springs it also has a unique micro-climate with mild winters (rarely falling below freezing) and very hot summers with daytime temperatures in the mid 30's and occasionally going above 40°C (42.7° has been recorded).

Ourense also became a strategic crossing point of the mighty Miño and its 3 tributaries which all flow through the town; the Barbaña, Loña and Barbañica. The famous Roman bridge *Ponte Romano* or *Ponte Vella (Roman foundations and rebuilt in the 12th and 17th centuries – see photo previous page)* is now in pedestrian use but the river has 10 bridges to carry the constant flow of traffic around its industrial and office hinterland. Ourense (formerly the ancient city of Auria or Aquis Aurensis) has been an administrative base for millennia; the Romans in the 1st century later occupied by the Suevi tribes in the 5th before being ransacked by the Moors (Al Mansur) in the 6th and rebuilt by the Alfonso III in the 7th. Sancho II and Doña Elvira (his sister) resettled the city in the 11th but it was in the 12th century that Ourense became established as a main centre of trade with pilgrims coming from the Via de la Plata and the Portuguese routes... and at the beginning of the 21st century we witness the renaissance of the camino de Sanabrés as it welcomes the new flow of pilgrims and acknowledged by the Xunta de Galicia with the renovation of a pilgrim hostel in the heart of the city centre (photo below).

■ **Historic Monuments & Places of Interest:** *(listed consecutively):* ❶ *As Burgas* historical hot spring with outdoor bath & fountain. ❷ *Xunta Albergue (photo>)* ❸ *Plaza Mayor & Concello*. ❹ *Catedral de San Martiño XII-XIII*c. ❺ *Iglesia de Santa Eufemia*. ❻ *Plaza Eugenio Montes Turismo* © 988 366 064 corner Rúa Isabel Católica 09:00-14:00 / 16:00-20:00 Sat & Sun: 11:00-14:00. Closed Tues. *www.turismodeourense.gal*

● *[250m off route* **Claustro de San Francisco** beautifully preserved cloisters from the 14th century adj. the small museum **Escolma De Escultura** with 18th century statue of Santiago Peregrino.

For the purpose of simplicity, lodging in the city can be divided into three main zones. Zone A in the historic town centre which includes the recently refurbished Xunta hostal conveniently located (within 100m) of the original Roman Baths (open to the public and open air) and the Praza Maior. ● *Alb.* **Ourense** *Xunta.[42÷4]* €8 ✆ 981 900 643 Rúa da Barreira, 12 (historic town centre adj. Plaza Mayor). ● *Alb.* **Grelo Hostel** *Priv.[32÷3]* €17 ✆ 988 614 564 *www.grelohostel.com* Rúa Peña Trevinca, 40 bajo (+450m from Plaza Mayor).

North of river: ● *Alb.* **Augas Quentes** *Priv.[36÷3]* €15 ✆ 988 061 322 [m] 679 958 780 *www.albergueaugasquentes.com* Rúa Vicente Risco, 34 (Roman Bridge +250m). Also •*Hs* **La Rotonda** *x20* €28-36 ✆ 988 607 759 *www.larotondahostalourense.com* Av. de Marín, 41 (+**500**m).

ZONE ❹ *(historic town centre)*: c/ Hermanos (Irmáns) Villar Nº15 ❶ *H* **Irixo** *x12* €35-50 ✆ 988 254 620. **Nº15b** ❷ *Hs* **Cándido** €40 ✆ 988 229 607. ❸ *H* **Zarampallo** €35-50 ✆ 988 230 008 *www.zarampallo.com* Nº19 (corner of S.Miguel above Rst. Kyoto). ❹ *H***Novo Cándido** *x12* €45-60 ✆ 988 989 125 *www.hotelnovocandido.com* Rúa San Miguel, 14. **ZONE ❺** *(inexpensive hostals close to the camino)*: c/ Papa Juan XXIII @Nº4 ❺ *Hs* **Lido** *x5* €27-37 ✆ 988 213 600 adj. @ Nº2 ❻ *H* **Miño** €35-45 ✆ 988 217 594. ❼ *H* **Corderi Rúa Ervedelo** @ Nº7 €25-35 ✆ 988 221 293 adj. ❽ **Ervedelo 7** €30-40 ✆ 988 238 152 above *café Ervedelo 7* opp. ❾ *H* **Altiana** €27-37 ✆ 988 370 952 *hotelaltiana.com* @ Nº14. **ZONE ❻** *(expensive hotels €60-€120 in modern quarter – see www.booking.com* : ❿ *H* **Gran Hotel San Martín** ✆ 988 371 811 Rúa M. Curros Enríquez, 1 adj. (now) ⓫ *H***Barceló Ourense.** ⓬ *H* **Princess** ✆ 2988 269 538 Av. da Habana, 45. ⓭ *H* **Carris Cardenal Quevedo** ✆ 988 375 523 Rúa Cardenal Quevedo, 28. ⓮ *H* **NH Ourense** ✆ 988 601 111 Rúa Celso Emilio Ferreiro, 24. ⓯ *H* **Francisco II** ✆ 988 242 095 c/ Juan Manuel Bedoya, 17. *[Note: Hotel Puente Romano is a misnomer and is 2.6 km south of the bridge!]*

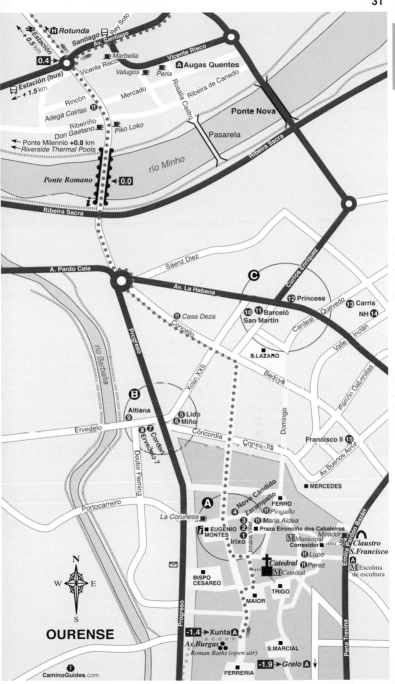

OURENSE

1 OURENSE – CEA *via Tamallancos*

108.2 km – Santiago

▥▥▥▥▥▥ --- ---		12.1 --- ---		55%
───── --- ---		8.3 --- ---		37%
───── --- ---		<u>1.8</u> --- ---		8%
Total km --- ---		**22.2** km (13.8 ml)		

▲ *equiv.* Ascent 1,410m (+7.1 =**29.3** km)

Alto.m ▲ Tamallancos 510m (1,670 ft)

<**Ⓐ Ⓗ**> Tamallancos **11.7** km *also*
Vidvedo 17.9 km Pazos **+** 0.7 km

Note: *Ourense–Cotelas (stage 2) 24.0 km*

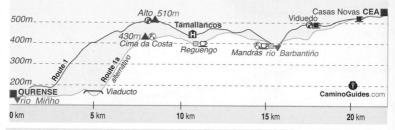

❏ **Mystical Path:** *Veni, vidi, vici. Julius Caesar.* The might of Rome and the arrogance that befalls all 'great' empires lead, inevitably, to their downfall. Today, as pilgrims, we come to learn in humility the lesson of unconditional Love. To the extent that we come to conquer, it is our own egoic and judgemental identity that we would destroy. The route ahead offers space to reflect on our true purpose for being here and now. Gratitude is the way of the pilgrim and we offer thanks for the positive aspects of a Rome that gave us the thermal baths in Ourense and the bridges which allow us to pass safely *Deo gratias*, but mindful they were built largely with enslaved labour.

❏ **Practical Path:** The main route commences with a very steep climb up to Tamallancos which offers a welcome break with cafés and lodging. The majority is via earth paths (55%) through ancient oak forest and views back over the Miñho valley. The alternative route by contrast is all by road to Cima da Costa alongside the N-130 before branching off along the OU-0520 with fast moving traffic on account of its straight and monotonous orientation. Both routes pass over the river Barbantiño by medieval single arch bridges before joining in Casas Novas for the final short stretch through oak woodland into Cea. ***Note:*** *If you are coming from the pilgrim albergue or other lodging in the old historic quarter around Plaza Mayor you need to add 1.4 km to Ponte Romano where measurements in this guide start (see town plan).*

0.0 km **Ponte Romano** Roman bridge over the majestic río Minho. Keep s/o to junction with the N-525 and **option [0.4 km]** *[!] [Note: many pilgrims inadvertently continue s/o at this point which is the* alternative *route via*

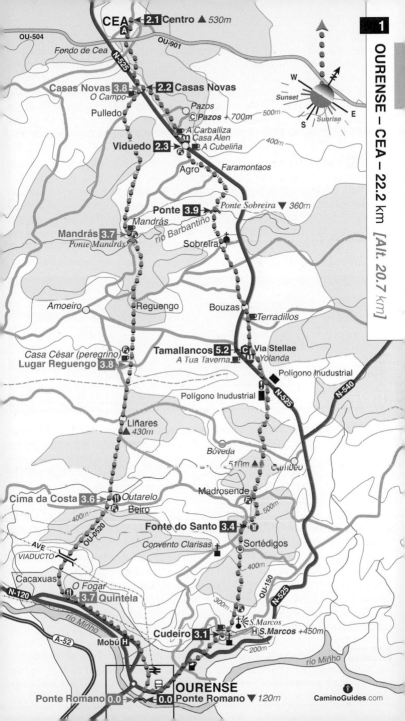

1

OU-504

CEA ◄ **2.1** Centro ▲ 530m
A

OU-901

Fondo de Cea

N-525

Sunset

W

E

S

Sunrise

500m

Casas Novas **3.8** ►◄ **2.2** Casas Novas
O Campo

Pulledo

Pazos
C **Pazos** + 700m

A Carballiza
m Casa Alen
Viduedo **2.3** ► ■ A Cubeliña
F

400m

Agro   Faramontaos

Ponte **3.9** ► Ponte Sobreira ▼ 360m
Mandrás

Mandrás **3.7** ► rio Barbantiño
Ponte Mandrás   Sobreira

Amoeiro   Reguengo   Bouzas

●Terradillos

Casa César (peregrino)   Tamallancos **5.2** ►C ► Via Stellae
Lugar Reguengo **3.8**   A Tua Taverna   m ●Yolanda

Polígono Inudustrial

Polígono Inudustrial   N-540

N-525

Liñares
▲430m

Bóveda

510m ▲   Camba

Madrosende

Cima da Costa **3.6** ► Outarelo
400m   F Beiro

OU-0520

Fonte do Santo **3.4** ► ■
AVE   Convento Clarisas ✝   Sortédigos
VIADUCTO

400m

Cacaxuas   OU-150   N-525
O Fogar
N-120 **3.7** Quintela   300m   QU-150

A-52   rio Miño   ✝ S.Marcos
Mobú H   Cudeiro **3.1** ► ■   H S.Marcos +450m

200m

rio Miño

OURENSE

Ponte Romano **0.0** ►◄ **0.0** Ponte Romano ▼ 120m   CaminoGuides.com

Reguengo – see page 38. An indistinct sign on the central reservation shows an arrow in both directions]. For the main route turn up right> into Avenida de Santiago past public toilets (right) with the balustrades of Parque da Ponte above. On the opp. side of the road is the bus-stop from/to Santiago *[Note: the main bus station is out in the suburbs 1.5 km to the west].* Continue up along the N-525 on wide pavements and turn off right> by service station **Cepsa [1.3** km] s/o over N-525*!* and up into **Cudeiro [0.4** km] on the OU-150.

3.1 km **Cudeiro** *Igrexa San Pedro A Terraza* opp. *Arco Vella* +500m •*H˚ San Marcos x12* €25-40 Ⓒ 988 511 655. Keep s/o up steeply past steps (right) to *Ermita S. Marcos* + 200m and viewpoint with **Fuente [0.6** km] *[F.].* Continue up into Sartédigos *[Detour right 1.5 km (3.0 km return!) to Igrexa de Santiago de Gustei XIIc.].* The ascent continues with modern building over to the left *Convento Clarisas de Vilar de Astrés.* We have a short 100m stretch on the busy OU-0526 before veering off right> into ancient oak woods and **option [0.5** km] (see photo below) to visit the enigmatic *Fonte de Santo (only 50m).*

3.4 km **Fonte do Santo** ancient moss covered fountain (water not drinkable) *50m off route* evocative of the medieval pilgrim period offering a quiet place for reflection. The track now becomes exposed rock as we enter the hamlet of Madrosende *[F.]* and continue alongside country lanes onto woodland path to an industrial estate *Polígono Industrial* where we cross *[!]* N-525 onto lane that brings us to the back of Tamallancos.

5.2 km **Tamallancos** *[F.]* small village *Rst.•H˚* **Via Stellae** *x5* €50-65 Ⓒ 988 279 649 *www.viastellae.com* with bar terrace. *Mini-Mercado Yolanda* (other side of the N-525) & *A Tua Taverna.* Continue by country lane into **Bouzas [0.8** km] *Rst.Terradillos.* Cross *[!]* N-525 onto track through woodland into the old hamlet of **Sobreira [2.2** km] past *O Peto de Animas* (right). *[Fine example (no longer extant) of these roadside shrines for the protection of the soul on its journey through purgatory].* We continue down to the fine one-arch medieval bridge over **río Barbantiño [0.9** km].

3.9 km **Ponte Sobreira** *[F.]* the ruins and the low lying path are often flooded in wet weather. We continue along a track into San Cristovo de Cea and up into **Aldea Faramontaos [0.8** km]. *[Detour s/o + 500m (1.0 km return) to several restaurants on N-525].* Turn left into **Viduedo [1.5** km] on N-525.

2.3 km **Viduedo** *[F.]* Cross *[!]* N-525 to *Bar A Cubeliña* and further out *mini-mercado Alen* adj. *café A Carballiza*. Just past this last cafe we take the path right> into oak woods to cross country lane and **option [0.7 km]** *[Detour 700m right to •CR Pazos x7 €45+ © 988 282 005 [m] 619 445 640 Paco. Renovated granite house in quiet hamlet].* At option point keep s/o along woodland track into **Casas Novas [1.5 km]**

2.2 km **Casas Novas** *café O Campo* (on *far* side of N-525). Keep s/o past *Forno da Maruja* onto path through woods past chicken farm and cross access road into Cea *Bar O Camiño* and under the main OU-504 bypass road where waymarks veer up right (or take short-cut s/o along grass track by river). Cross over bridge and enter the old town, pass access lane (left) to albergue and turn up right at crossroads to Plaza Mayor in Cea town centre.

2.1 km **Cea Centro** Spacious main square dominated by a granite clock tower and the somewhat austere council offices *Concello* readily identified with their flags. *Bar Plaza* spills out onto the square and gets the evening sun and at the lower end of the square is *café O Vatican*. Off  the main square near the Concello (rear of Pescado O Gove) is *•CR* **Mañoso** *x5* €40-50 © 687 932 467 / 637 068 412 *www.casamanoso.es* Rúa Campo da Feira where Roberto & Antía welcome guests to their rural idyll. The pilgrim hostel *Casa das Netas* is a well renovated stone building occupying a tranquil part of the old village in the lower part of town on c/ Santo Cristo. ● *Alb.* **de peregrinos de Cea** *Xunta [44÷2]* €8 © 988 282 000 [m] 600 878 289. *Note: next albergue with private rooms in Cotelas only 1.9 km (see next stage).*

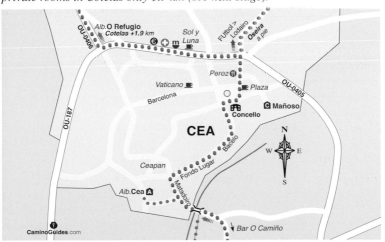

CEA: Traditional village with good facilities including several cafés and restaurants located around the central clock tower (see photo>). The main street has supermarket, chemist, bank and *panaderias* selling the local bread for which it is famous. Cea has been baking bread using the same basic ingredients and methods since the thirteenth century and has its own D.O. *denominación de origen* to protect the quality of the product.

OPTION next stage: *Cea to Castro Dozón via* **Cotelas** *or* **Oseira***?* From Cea we have the option to continue via the alternative route to visit the remote Oseira Monastery (see next stage).

REFLECTIONS: *Did I come, see and conquer my prejudices today or did I allow them run rampant?*

_____
_____
_____
_____
_____
_____
_____
_____
_____
_____
_____
_____
_____
_____
_____
_____
_____
_____
_____
_____
_____
_____

Ponte Sobreira   medieval bridge over the río Barbantiño

1a **OURENSE – CEA** *via Reguengo*
108.2 km – Santiago

┄┄┄┄┄	--- ---	8.2	--- ---	*40%*
─────	--- ---	9.5	--- ---	*46%*
─────	--- ---	<u>3.0</u>	--- ---	*14%*
Total km	--- ---	**20.7 km** (12.9 ml)		

▲ *equiv.* Ascent 1,250m (+6.2 =**26.9** km)
Alto.*m* ▲ Cea 550m (1,805 ft)
< A H > None.
Note: Ourense–Cotelas (stage 2) 22.5 km

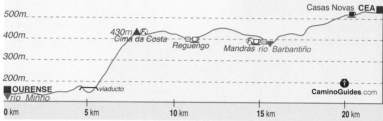

See Stage 1 map p.33. Note if you are coming from the pilgrim albergue in Ourense or other lodging in the old historic quarter around Plaza Mayor you need to add 1.4 km to Ponte Romano where measurements in this guide start (see town plan). Note also that there are few facilities on this route and they may be closed early in the day. Take energy snacks and water.

0.0 km **Ponte Romano** Keep s/o to junction with N-525 and **option [0.4 km]** *! [Note: The main route via Tamallancos turns up right at this junction].* Keep s/o up Av. de las Caldas past popular •*Hs****La Rotonda** *x20* €28-36 Ⓒ 988 607 759 *www.larotondahostalourense.com* corner of Av. de Marín 41 opp. **rail station [0.3 km]**. We follow the line of the railway s/o at playpark *[F.]* alongside the N-120 on wide pavement past •*H** **Mabú** *x28* €25-40 Ⓒ 988 217 842 *www.hotelmabu.com* to veer up right at *Rst. O Fogón sign* **Quintela [3.0 km]**.

3.7 km **Quintela** *Rst. O Fogón* start of the U-0520 Km '0' as we pass through industrial estate *polígono industrial Rst. Coto do Rano* (up right) and drop down sharply under AVE rail viaduct (photo>) *[F.]* (left). The road ahead is somewhat daunting as it climbs steeply in a monotonous straight line and while traffic is infrequent it tends

Paso elevado del AVE

to be fast moving and the road is narrow along the Costiña de Canedo. We finally arrive at the summit.

3.6 km Cima da Costa *cruce [F.]* (right) *Castro de Beiro / A Abelaira.* We keep s/o past *Rst. Outarela* (right) and tienda (left) *Daniels neither of which is likely to be open for pilgrims in the early morning.* At the end of the village we veer off left onto a track through ancient oak woods which offer shelter from sun or rain (!) and then back onto asphalt road as we enter the Concello Amoeiro. Keep s/o at Liñares crossroads over dry river basin and veer off right onto track before entering the hamlet of Lugar Reguengo.

3.8 km Reguengo a warm welcome awaits at *Casa César* a colourful pilgrim stop *parada de peregrino.* César is one of those legendary characters that add so much charm to the road. He is ably abetted by Felicidad who helps dole out the alcohol and local fare, coffee or tea may be available. It is primarily a place to swap pilgrim stories, memorabilia and photos! *[F.]* (left).

3.7 km Ponte Mandrás We now enter a remote and beautiful stretch of ancient oak forest along a shaded path that ends abruptly at the medieval bridge over the río Barbantiño in Mandrás. *[F.]* (right) and *Bar Mandrás.* We enter into oak woods again through the hamlet of Pulledo and up to the main road N-525.

3.8 km Casas Novas *Bar O Campo* (left). Cross *[!]* the N-525 and turn imm. left (main route joins from the right) and proceed past *Forno da Maruja* onto path through woods past chicken farm (noisy dogs) and cross access road into **Cea** *Bar O Camiño* and under the main OU-504 bypass road where waymarks veer up right (or take short-cut s/o along grass track by river). Cross over bridge and enter the old town, past access lane (left) to •*Alb.***Cea** and turn up right at crossroads to Plaza Mayor in the centre of town.

2.1 km Cea Centro All facilities (see page 33).

Reflections / Notes: use previous page.

2 CEA – CASTRO DOZÓN
via COTELAS

86.0 km – Santiago

ıııııııııııı	--- ---	7.2	--- ---	47%
▬▬▬▬	--- ---	7.3	--- ---	48%
▬▬▬	--- ---	0.7	--- ---	5%
Total km	--- ---	**15.2** km (9.4 ml)		

equiv. ▲ Ascent 980m (+4.9 =**20.1** km)
Alto.m ▲ High Moors 860m (2,822 ft)
<🅰 🅷> Cotelas **1.8** km / O Reino **6.7**+
*Casarello **+1.3** / Note:* Cea–Estación de Lalín (stage 3) **28.3** km

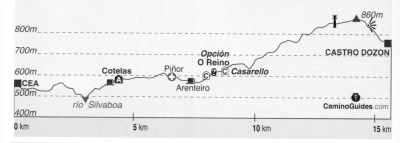

Where are you headed for? It takes so many thousand years to wake, but will you wake for pity's sake. Christopher Frye *A Sleep of Prisoners.*

❏ **Mystical Path:** It is only yesterday when we left the busyness of city life around Ourense but already the unhurried life of rural Galicia exerts its quiet influence. Today our choice is the emptiness of high moorland around Monte de San Martino or the remote valley of the lowland around the monastery in Oseira. Both offer an opportunity to walk in the silence of nature and to reflect on what really matters in life. Are we part of the emerging woke society where going back to sleep is no longer an option. Are we headed for a Compostela or some other, deeper acknowledgement and destination that has not quite materialised in our mind?

❏ **Practical Path:** A short stage but with a steep climb towards the end pushing the modest 15.2 km to a more demanding equivalent of 19.8 km. The first section to O Reino option point is mostly road but the latter half is across lovely open moorland with fine views over high scrub-land. There are *no* facilities from Arenteiro so take plenty of water and energy snacks. If you are staying in the albergue note it is 400m *off* route further along the N-525. If you plan to cook in the hostel you can buy food at the *Goviran* mini-market or take the *menú* in café Canton. No other facilities.

0.0 km Cea *Centro* From the clock-tower (add 300m from the albergue) keep s/o by *café Plaza* past *Pulperia Perez* (note discrete waymark imm.

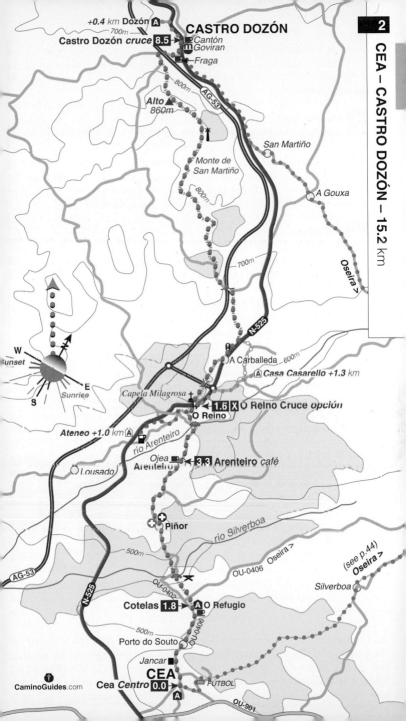

CASTRO DOZÓN

+0.4 km Dozón [A]
700m
Castro Dozón *cruce* 8.5

Cantón
Goviran
Fraga

AG-53

800m

Alto
860m

San Martiño

Monte de
San Martiño

A Gouxa

800m

Oseira >

700m

N-525

600m

A Carballeda

[A] *Casa Casarello +1.3 km*

Capela Milagrosa

1.6 [X] O Relno Cruce *opción*

O Reino

Ateneo +1.0 km [A]
río Arenteiro

Ojea
Arenteiro

3.3 Arenteiro *café*

Lousado

Piñor

río Silverboa

Oseira >

500m

OU-0406

(see p.44)
Oseira >

AG-53

OU-0402

Silverboa

N-525

Cotelas 1.8 [A] O Refugio

500m

Porto do Souto
OU-0406

Jancar

CEA
Cea Centro 0.0 >
[A]

FÚTBOL

OU-901

W
Sunset
S
E
Sunrise

opp.) and at roundabout [50m] turn left down the main street (the *pedestrian* way to Oseira is s/o up) and at the bottom turn right signposted Oseira (*road* route OU-406) and continue past *Jancar* showrooms (left) through **Porto do Souto** into **Cotelas**.

1.8 km **Cotelas** ●*Alb./Rst*. **O Refugio** *Priv. [12÷4]* €8+ ✆ 988 282 593 [m] 606 709 167 (Antonio) *www.orefugio.es* lugar Cotelas. Welcoming new hostel with dormitory / private rooms, restaurant and small shop. *Rst.Nova Lua* (+300m along main road). Continue to the rear of the hostel onto path over río Silverboa with picnic benches by bridge *area recreativa* and *[F.]* (right by old bridge). Keep s/o into **Piñor [1.9** km] with ✚ Farmacia, Concello, Centro Saude. Keep s/o by road through Fontelo into **Arenteiro [1.2** km].

3.3 km **Arenteiro** *café Ojea (last opportunity for refreshment before reaching Castro Dozón 10.1 km)*. Continue past *capela da Peregrina* down to bridge over *río Arenteiro* in **A Ponte [1.0** km] and turn up right off road onto path and cross over secondary road **OU-154 [0.3** km] in **O Reino** and first of two options to Ateneo (see below). Cross over onto concrete path up to the main road **N-525 [0.3** km] by Anduriña office.

1.6 km **O Reino** *opción N-525*. ▲

[Detour ❶ *1.0 km (2.0 km return)* ● ● ● ● ● *Rst.•Hs Ateneo* €25+ ✆ 988 403 203 *on N-525. Directions: where the path crosses the OU-154 turn down left along it and keep s/o at staggered crossroads [200m] signposted Lousada and take next right [200m] and turn left along the busy N-525 [100m] [!]. Keep to the margin facing oncoming traffic to Cepsa filling station and wait until the road is clear in both directions and cross over [!] to the hotel [400m].*

[Detour ❷ *1.3 km (no need to return – continue on to rejoin waymarked route in Carballeda).* ● ● ● ● ●*•CR Casa Casarellos x8* €45-60 *incl. breakfast* ✆ 988 403 222 *www.casarellos.es Casarellos. Luxury accommodation with swimming pool. Owner will drive guests to nearby restaurant if dinner required].* Directions: At option point  turn up right along the N-525 and right at roundabout [350m] and imm. left [50] sign Turismo Rural Casarellos and continue along quiet country lane to Casarellos [900m].*

▲ To continue on the waymarked route cross the N-525 *[!]* and turn up sharp left with *capela de Milagrosa* (left 50m) and turn right onto track that continues over the AG-53 access road and back down to the **N-525 [1.0** km] where the alternative route from Casa Casarello joins from the right. We now have a 500m stretch of the busy main road before turning off left onto a delightful track that continues for over 6 km over high moorland to the outskirts of Castro Dozón passing out of Ourense province into Pontevedra. We cross a small river onto a stretch through mixed woodland to cross over the **AG-53 [1.6** km]. We now begin the climb up onto the open moorland with farm building visible in the far distance. Pass **radio mast [3.5** km] (right) the only other sign of human activity in this wonderfully open and windswept environment. We now pass the high point of this stage at 860m before dropping down with fine views over the surrounding countryside with the motorway snaking its way towards Castro Dozón. Cross the AG-53 up to the **N-525 [2.2** km] and welcome *café Fraga*. Turn left down to **bus shelter [0.2** km] by side road and *café Cantón* in **Castro Dozón**.

8.5 km **Castro Dozón** *café Cantón menú / mini-mercado Coviran* (shop if you plan to cook in the albergue). The hostel is visible from here +400m further along the N-525. ●*Alb.* **Castro Dozón** *Mun. [44÷3]* €6 *x3* €10 (ind.) ℂ 687 058 612 (Cristina) individual beds can be reserved in advance. Return to option point at café Cantón to proceed.

REFLECTIONS:

2a CEA – CASTRO DOZÓN
via OSEIRA

70.8 km – Santiago

┈┈┈┈┈┈	--- ---	10.5	--- ---	*52%*
————	--- ---	7.4	--- ---	*37%*
▬▬▬▬	--- ---	<u>2.1</u>	--- ---	*11%*
Total km		**20.1** km (12.5 ml)		

▰▰ *equiv.* Ascent 1,150m (+5.7=**25.8** km)
Alto.m ▲ Above Oseira 830m (2,725 ft)
< Ⓐ Ⓗ > Oseira **9.0** km.

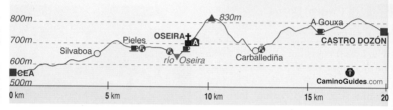

❏ **Practical Path:** This alternative stage via Oseira is 4.6 km longer but with the opportunity to visit and stay in the monastery complex. Note that while 52% is via delightful paths over the hills into and out of Oseira nevertheless we end up with 2.2 km of hard slog along the verge of the busy N-525 running parallel with the AG-53 into Castro Dozón. Waymarks are generally good but there are a few places in the dense woodland out of Cea where you need to stay focussed.

0.0 km **Cea** *Centro* From the clocktower (add 300m from the albergue) keep s/o by *café Plaza* past *Pulperia Perez* (note waymark imm. opp.) and at roundabout [50m] continue s/o up signposted *Campo de Fútbol*). Continue to rear of **football ground [0.4** km] (option here to join the main route via OU-406 down left) and continue into ancient oak woods on a quiet path with occasional sections of the old granite track followed by pilgrims and monks since medieval times. We emerge from the woods onto **asphalt road [3.8** km] into **Silverboa [0.3** km] population 2! *[F.]* (left – tap on wall). Continue by quiet road into **Pieles [1.7** km].

6.2 km **Pieles** *[F.]* (right) *café O Toxo*. Turn right at crossroads over río Pieles through **A Ventala [1.3** km] (church with adj. shelter down right). Keep s/o past *[F.]* (right) and over the river and up past the side of the monastery into the centre of **Oseira [0.5** km].

2.8 km **Oseira** quaint village centred around the monastic buildings in peaceful valley setting. Several cafés adj. the monastery *café Venezuela* and *café Escudo* the latter with a coat of arms above the door with the date 1622.
●*Alb.***Monasterio de Oseira** *Conv.* *[40÷1]* €8 ✆ 988 282 004. An austere

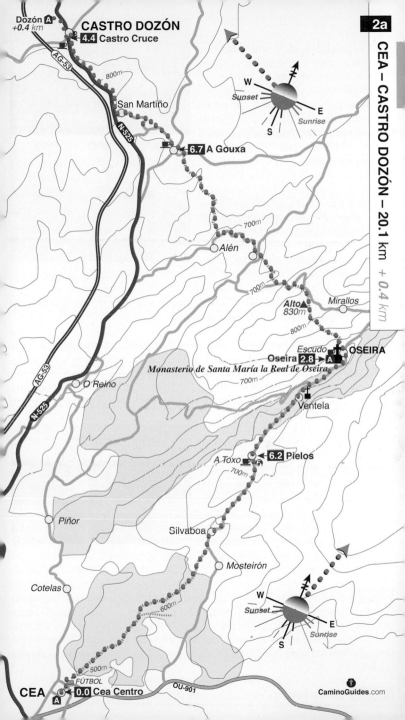

Dozón **A**
+0.4 km

CASTRO DOZÓN

4.4 Castro Cruce

AG-53

800m

N-525

San Martiño

6.7 A Gouxa

W — Sunset

E — Sunrise

S

700m

Alén

700m

Alto ▲
830m

Mirallos

800m

Escudo
Oseira **2.8** **A** **OSEIRA**

Monasterio de Santa María la Real de Oseira

700m

O Reino

AG-53

N-525

Ventela

6.2 Pielos

A Toxo

700m

Piñor

Silvaboa

Mosteirón

Cotelas

W — Sunset

E — Sunrise

S

600m

500m

CEA

FÚTBOL

A **0.0** Cea Centro

OU-901

CaminoGuides.com

building with basic accommodation and kitchenette with vending machine. Pilgrims are welcome to join in the religious services of this Cistercian community now reduced to around a dozen monks. The monastery of **Santa María la Real de Oseira** was founded in the twelfth century originally by Benedictine monks but passing to the Cistercian Order, following the strict Trappist discipline. The monastery is open for spiritual retreat of not less than 2 days *www.hosderia@ mosteirodeoseira.org* and does not accept pilgrims simply travelling through for which the pilgrim hostel

is available (see previous page). The monumental buildings gave rise to the sobriquet *El Escorial Gallego* after the vast 16th century Renaissance royal palace complex near Madrid. The adj. church was built in the 17th century with a Baroque facade and Gothic elements.

Guided tours are available and there is a small monastery shop selling, amongst other specialties, the famous liquor called *Eucaliptine* made exclusively here to a recipe known only to the monks. There are two varieties: Amber: a combination of 3 species of eucalyptus and Gold: mixing several medicinal plants including Melissa, Chamomile, Hyssop, Peppermint, Angelica, Cocoa, Artemis, Elderflower and Clove!

We continue along the traditional cobbled street and up a concrete path that shortly afterwards becomes a narrow path with lovely views back over Oseira. We now reach the high point *Alto* at 830m. The path decends to cross a road into **Vilarello** (no services) and down into **Carballediña** [3.5 km] *[F.]* (left). We continue out of the village by road and turn up right onto path and down into the province of Pontevedra and **A Gouxa** [3.2 km].

6.7 km **A Gouxa** just beyond crossroads we find the somewhat neglected *Bar/Rst.* the first opportunity for refreshment since leaving Oseira. Despite its run down appearance it serves a hearty menú del dia. Keep s/o through the hamlet of **Bidueiros** and into **San Martiño** [2.1 km] this is the point we emerge onto the **busy N-525** which we follow all the way into **Castro Dozón** [2.2 km].

4.4 km **Castro Dozón** *café Cantón* (see stage2 for list of services).

REFLECTIONS:

Monasterio de Santa María la Real de Oseira

3 CASTRO DOZÓN – A LAXE

70.8 km – Santiago

::::::::::::::::::::	--- ---	9.0	--- ---	*47%*
————	--- ---	8.0	--- ---	*41%*
▬▬▬▬	--- ---	<u>2.3</u>	--- ---	*12%*
Total km	--- ---	**19.3** km (12.0 ml)		

equiv. Ascent 830m (+4.1 =**23.4** km)

Alto.m ▲ Dozón 780m (2,560 ft)

< Ⓐ Ⓗ > Estación de Lalín **13.1**

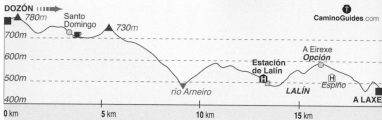

"The road goes ever on and on, down from the door where it began... and I must follow, if I can... Until it joins some larger way where many paths and errands meet. And whither then? I cannot say" J.R.R. Tolkien.

❏ **Mystical Path:** Today we descend towards A Laxe where we join pilgrims coming from the camino Invierno. We travel together to Santiago but where do we go from there? Santiago is not the end of the journey but a new point of departure. Is our final journey the end of this world and earthly existence. The Land of Eternal Youth *Tir na Nóg* lies over the horizon... and where to then? I travel now with ever more resolve to meet the inner Guide who alone can point the way...

❏ **Practical Path:** This is another relatively short stage and most of it downhill as we descend from 780m to 470m. Services along the way are few and far between with *Estación de Lalín* offering a good midway refuelling point. Take water and energy snacks and, if you are blessed with sunshine, take precautions against the sun as shade is in short supply. If you don't wish to stay in the albergue in A Laxe there is an option to take a detour to join the route from Lalín at Espiño 1.6 km. If you wish to visit Lalín you can backtrack from here along the lovely river path (see stage 08). Alternatively there is the Hotel & Spa at Pazo de Bendoiro 1.7 km beyond (see next stage).

0.0 km **Castro Dozón** *Cruce* (Add 0.4 km if you are staying at the albergue). Take the secondary road by *café Cantón* and continue past Igrexa de San Salvador and up to an isolated new industrial estate before dropping down to the N-525. A somewhat indistinct access to a path through the woodland ahead runs parallel to the main road for ½ km before returning to

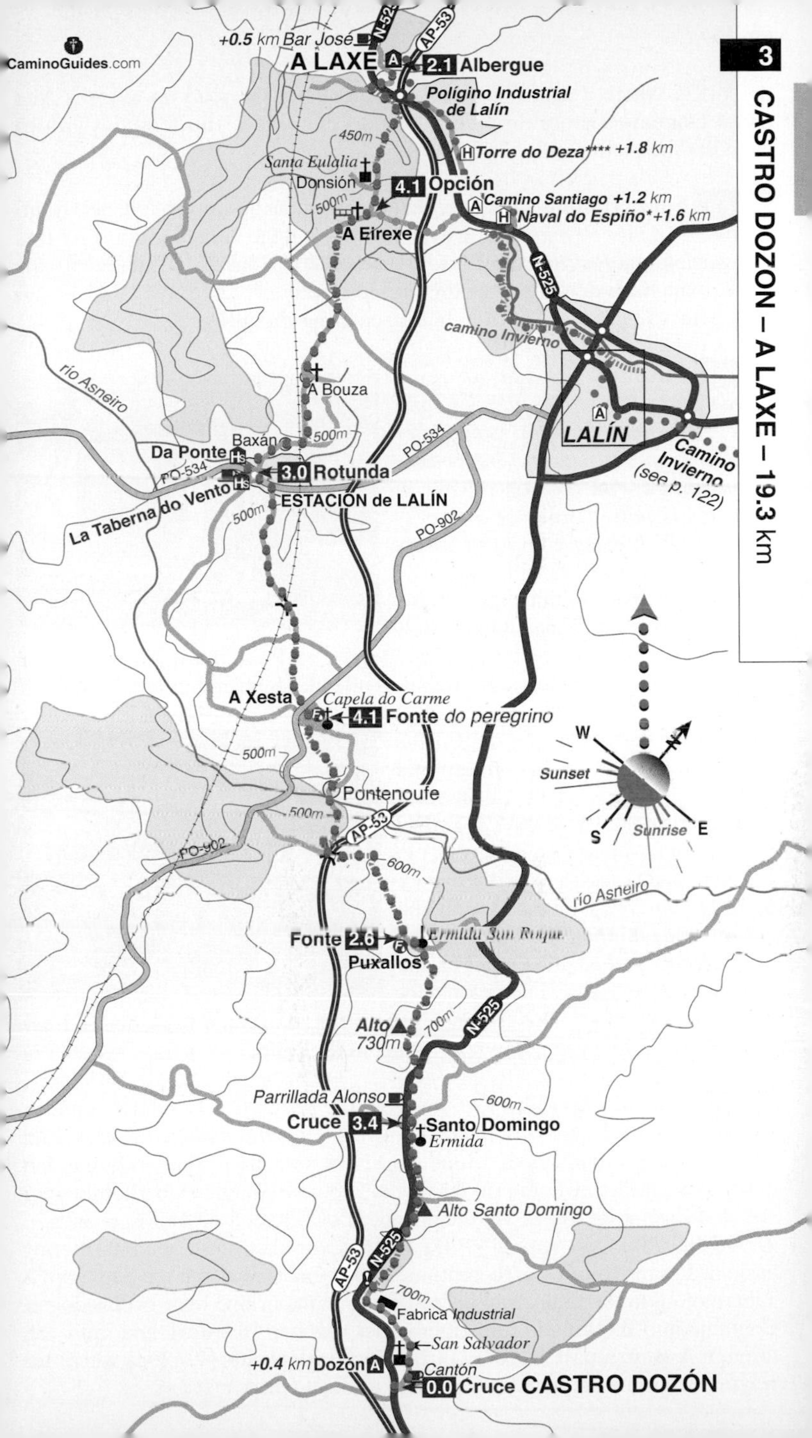

+0.5 km Bar José

A LAXE Ⓐ ✈ **2.1 Albergue**

Políginio Industrial de Lalín

Ⓗ*Torre do Deza**** +1.8 km*

450m

Santa Eulalia ✝
Donsión **4.1 Opción**

500m Ⓐ *Camino Santiago +1.2 km*
Ⓗ *Naval do Espiño* +1.6 km*

A Eirexe ✝

N-525

camino Invierno

✝
A Bouza

500m

PO-534

Da Ponte **Baxán**

PO-534
3.0 Rotunda

La Taberna do Vento ✝ ✝

ESTACIÓN de LALÍN

Ⓐ **LALÍN**

Ⓐ **Camino Invierno** *(see p. 122)*

500m

PO-902

✝

A Xesta *Capela do Carme*

✝ **4.1 Fonte** *do peregrino*

500m

Pontenoufe

AP-53

600m

río Asneiro

Fonte 2.6 Ⓡ *Ermida San Roque*

Puxallos

Alto ▲
730m N-525

Parrillada Alonso

Cruce 3.4 ✝ **Santo Domingo**
Ermida

600m

▲ *Alto Santo Domingo*

700m

AP-53 N-525

🏭
Fábrica Industrial

✝ ←*San Salvador*

+0.4 km **Dozón** Ⓐ *Cantón*

◄ 0.0 Cruce CASTRO DOZÓN

W ☼ N E
Sunset
S *Sunrise* E

the N-525 where a path (of sorts) runs alongside the road up towards Alto Santo Domingo before dropping down to the village (no facilities) which straddles the main road.

3.4 km **Santo Domingo** the only feature being the diminutive chapel (right) *Ermida de Santo Domingo* However, just beyond the village (300m) we find the welcoming *Parrillada Alonso*. Another 400m takes us finally off the N-525 which we don't meet again until just before A Laxe. We climb to our high point of this stage at 730m before entering **Puxallos**.

2.6 km **Puxallos** *Ermida de San Roque*. [San Roque the pilgrim saint with staff and shell is sometimes mistaken for St. James but easily distinguished with the dog always at heel. He is patron saint of a variety of causes incl. disease and the falsely accused... as well as pilgrims and dogs!]. [F.]. We continue out of the hamlet onto a track that winds itself  over the motorway and down to the hamlet of **Pontenoufe** with its stone bridge over the río Asneiro. It's then a gentle climb up and into **A Xesta**.

4.1 km **A Xesta** *Capela do Carme* [F.] *Fonte do Peregrino* and traditional house displaying artefacts of the rural farming community *Casa do Patrón Museo Etnográfico*. A Xesta is the starting point for a circular walk *Sendeiro da Xesta* based around the camino and taking in local sights incl. the Capela S. Roque, the Gran Mámoa no Couto do Correlo and the ancient  bridge at Pontenoufe. We continue out of the village and back onto a track and over the railway and down to **Estación de Lalín.**

3.0 km **Estación de Lalín** We now join the busy PO-534 which connects the railway station here with the main town itself **Lalín** 4 km to the east. Turn left down to the roundabout 150m and *either* turn sharp right and imm. left down to the bridge over the río Ríadogos 250m *or* continue s/o 100m to *café* •*Hs* **A Taberna de Vento** visible ahead on c/ Estación de Botos *x7* €25-35 ✆ 986 780 734. Opp. *cafe* & •*P* **Da Ponte** somewhat run-down but offering basic bedrooms from €15. To continue make your way down the path opp. A Taberna to join the main waymarked route at the bridge over río Ríadogos. Continue into **Baxán** and turn right under **rail line [0.8 km].** and imm. left through **A Bouza** past *cruceiro* in **Botos** to **crossroads [1.7 km]** where the waymarked route continues s/o to track through oak woods.

*[**Detour Lalín**: note this is the closest point to Lalín town centre with its variety of restaurants, hotels and albergue. It lies 3.4 km due east and can be accessed (no signage) by turning right at the crossroads and continuing over the AP-53 past Ceminteiro da Romea (left) and Estadio Manuel Cortizon (right) into Av. Montserrat and s/o over N-525 and down past the bus station into the centre of town (see town plan and facilities on stage 08 of the Camino Invierno route p.127). Continue to A Laxe via the picturesque river walk also described on stage 08].*

We emerge from the oak woods onto secondary road into **A Eirexe [1.4** km].

4.1 km **A Eirexe** *Iglesia Santa Eulalia* fine roadside *cruceiro* and *Taberna Ruta de la Plata* & rest area. Keep s/o out of the village for 200m and turn left

▲ *[Note this is another option point to continue s/o (not the waymarked route left) to join the Camino Invierno for additional accommodation around Lalín industrial estate. A signpost here directs to the Hostal Camino de Santiago which is now 1.2 km on the N-525. However, the hostal was recently closed and it is not clear when or if it will reopen so the sign may be removed. However, other lodging in the area is listed under stage 08. To access keep s/o and continue over the motorway and directly down to the N-525 (Hostal Camino de Santiago in front). Turn down right to •Hostal **do Espiño** where the Invierno route join and waymarks continue to the rear of the hostal].*

▲Turn left at option and continue past the turning to **Donisón** (*not* Dozón) onto track through dense woodland up to the side of the AP-53 where pilgrims have made crucifixes out of branches of trees and placed these on the metal fencing along the motorway. Continue steeply down the side of the motorway onto secondary road to take a dangerous crossing over the busy N-525 *[!]*. Wait until traffic is clear in both directions before attempting to cross. Continue on the secondary road over the small stream that runs along the low-lying valley floor with reference to mosquitoes in its name *Rego da Laxe dos Mosqueiros* to the albergue in A Laxe.

2.1 km **A Laxe** ● *Alb.de Peregrinos* **A Laxe** *Xunta [30÷2]* €8. modern interior with all facilities built into a traditional stone building at the point were the caminos Invierno and Sanabrés meet. There are no other facilities at this point but pilgrims tend to congregate for food and drink at *bar José* on the N-525 a further 500m beyond the hostel up a paved access

road. If you are looking for a gourmet meal you can continue a further 1.0 km to Pazo do Bendoiro (1.5 km from the albergue) which also has luxury rooms (see next stage). Population of A Laxe 100. Lalín 20,100!

4 A LAXE – PONTE ULLA

51.5 km – Santiago

▓▓▓▓▓▓▓	--- ---	**10.8**	--- ---	*36%*
━━━━━	--- ---	**16.9**	--- ---	*57%*
▬▬▬▬▬	--- ---	<u>2.1</u>	--- ---	*7%*

Total km --- --- **29.8 km** (18.5 ml)

equiv. Ascent 1,190m (+5.9=**35.7** km)

Alto.m ▲ Silleda 520m (1,705 ft)

< Ⓐ Ⓗ > Ponte Taboada **4.6** km –
Trasfontao **7.5** km– Silleda km **9.4** – Bandeira **16.6** km – Dornelas **21.5** km

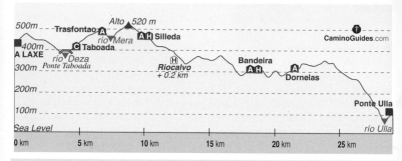

We have yet to learn the simple act of walking the earth like brothers.
Martin Luther King Jr.

❏ **Mystical Path:** We begin today at the point where the Winter Way joins the Way from Sanabrés. Both, in turn, connecting with a larger network of caminos. The camino Invierno connects us with the camino Francés with links to the whole of Europe. Sanabrés links us to the Via de la Plata and camino Mozarabe and, indirectly, to North Africa. In fact the camino is unique because it links us to every nation on earth. Not even the United Nations can claim to have adherents from every corner of our world. A Laxe is such a quiet and humble meeting point, in stark contrast to the motorways which hem it in. Today our path will see our camino family extended. Take time to connect and extend a loving smile...expecting nothing in return.

❏ **Practical Path:** Pilgrims from both the caminos Invierno and Sanabrés now continue together so we have an opportunity to welcome our expanding camino family. This is a relatively long stage but it is mostly downhill and can be shortened at a variety of interim stops... or indeed extended by continuing to the albergue in Outeiro (see stage 5). Note the large swathes of forest which now turns from ancient oak woods to commercial pine and eucalyptus as we approach Santiago.

0.0 km **A Laxe** *Albergue* Take the steep cobbled lane up to the N-525 and cross over *[!]* and just beyond *Rst. José* veer left onto lane that becomes a

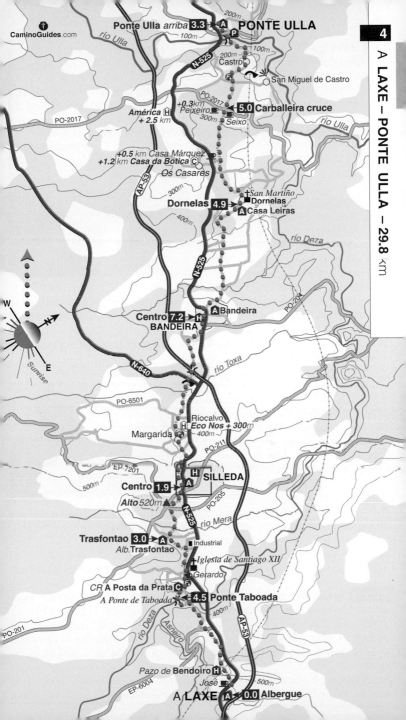

Ponte Ulla *arriba* **3.3** ⒶⓅ **PONTE ULLA**
200m
100m
río Ulla
N-525
100m
200m
Castro
San Miguel de Castro
CaminoGuides.com
PO-2017
PO-2017
+0.3km **5.0 → Carballeira cruce**
América Ⓗ *Peixeiro* 300m
+ 2.5 km *Seixo*
AP-53
+0.5 km Casa Márquez
+1.2 km Casa da Botica Ⓒ
Os Casares
300m
†San Martiño
■ **Dornelas**
Dornelas 4.9 → Ⓐ **Casa Leiras**
400m
río Deza
PO-204
Centro 7.2 Ⓗ Ⓐ **Bandeira**
BANDEIRA
N-540
río Toxa
PO-6501
Ⓗ *Riocalvo*
Margarida Ⓐ *Eco Nos + 300m*
400m
PO-211
EP-201
Ⓗ **SILLEDA**
500m
Ⓐ
Centro 1.9
Alto 520m ▲
N-525
PO-205
río Mera
Trasfontao 3.0 → Ⓐ
Alb.Trasfontao
■ *Industrial*
■ *Iglesia de Santiago XII*
■ *Gerardo*
CR A Posta da Prata Ⓒ
A Ponte de Taboada ✕ **← 4.5 Ponte Taboada**
400m
AP-53
río Deza
Asneiro
PO-201
Pazo de Bendoiro Ⓗ
José ■
500m
A LAXE Ⓐ **0.0 Albergue**
EP-6004

track and keep s/o to **crossroads** [1.5 km]. *Detour left 150m* to luxury spa hotel and restaurant •*H* **Pazo de Bendoiro** *x12* €65-75 © 986 794 289 *www. pazodebendoiro.com* Bendoiro de Abaixo +150m. Continue along N-525 for 200m before veering off left onto path and then a lane down to road bridge over the río Deza. We now have one of the most quintessential sections of the camino; a delightful track through ancient oak woods following the course of the river Deza down to the picturesque **A Ponte de Taboada [3.0** km].

4.5 km **Ponte Taboada** Magnificent stone bridge dating back to 912 (recorded in the Latin inscription on the bridge) with a single pointed arch. It replaced an earlier Roman bridge and is evidence of the itinerary of the Via da Plata and its historical passage over the river Deza. Continue on the original stone path passing access to •*CR* **Casa A Posta da Prata** *x6* €65 © 986 580 011 [m] 648 186 318 Lugar A Ponte Taboada. We alternate between track and quiet country lanes up to N-525. Just before the main road we find the traditional *Taberna A Casa de Gerardo* [1.2 km] with quiet patio to the rear *[F.]* (right). Continue along the N-525 on dangerous bend *[!]* keep *this* side *facing* the oncoming traffic for 100m and turn up left into woodland track▲.

[Note at this point there is an option to visit the 12th century Romanesque church of **Santiago de Taboada** *on the* **far** *side of the road. Worthy of a visit but take extra care in crossing [!]. Note the tympanum over entrance door and polychrome depiction of Santiago Matamoros at the battle of Clavijo situated over the main altar. We also find a statue of the pilgrim saint San Roque and a motif of Samson and the lion. An attentive volunteer stamps credenciales and there is a water font [F.]].*

▲ Follow the delightful path through oak woods that lead to the edge of an industrial estate before veering back into the woods to **Trasfontao [1.8** km].

3.0 km **Trasfontao** traditional hamlet with impressive 17th century Pazo de Trasfontao opp. ● *Alb. Turístico* **Trasfontao** *Priv. [10÷1]* €10 +*1* €30-40 © 650 261 774 / 666 704 403. Dinner available and small bar, terrace and swim pool. Continue over the río Mera and up to our high point of this stage at 520m just before entering the busy town of **Silleda** by a new block of apartments (right). The waymarked route turns left at this point along Rua Santa Eulalia ◆ *[Detour right 200m along Rúa Carballeira do Chousiño to new hostal and restaurant Casas Novas on the main N-535* •*Hs.Rst.* **Casa**

Novas *x26* €23-27 ℂ 86 580 898 *Barrio do Campo, 19].* ◆ Turn left on the main road and keep s/o along Rua Santa Eulalia to the handsome stone church in the centre of town.

1.9 km **Silleda** *Centro Igrexa de Santa Eulalia* (see town map). Town population 3,500. Lodging is plentiful which results in ample inexpensive options. Adjoining the church in the centre of town is: ❶ *Alb.***Santa Olaia** *Par. [48÷15]+* €8 (€5 in *pavillion*) ℂ 986 580 013/ 646 718 015 *www.booking. com* Av. del Parque 17. It is easy to get lost in the town, with its many busy thoroughfares, but most accommodation is north of the town centre ± 500m. ❷*Alb. Turístico* **Silleda** *Priv. [20÷1]* €10 *+6* €20-25 ℂ 986 580 192 *www. albergueturisticosilleda.es* c/Venezuela, 38. ❸ **El Gran Albergue Silleda** *Priv. [20÷2]* €10 *+4* €20 ℂ 986 580 156 c/Antón Alonso Ríos, 18. Other hostals and hotels: *Hs** **Toxa** *x6* €15 ℂ 986 580 111 c/Trasdeza, 88. •*Hs*** **Bluû** *x7* €20+ ℂ 986 580 156 c/Antón Alonso Ríos, 20. •*H** **Ramos** *x36* €35-45 ℂ 986 581 212 *www.hotelramos.com* c/San Isidro, 24. •*Hs* **Pardo** *x3* €25+ ℂ 986 580 965. •*H********Vía Argentum** *x88* €44-49 ℂ 986 581 330 *www. hotelviaargentum.com* c/Outeiro *+0.9 km*

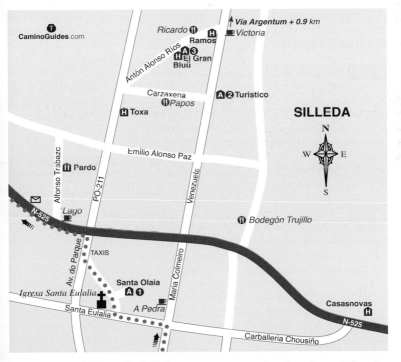

From *Igrexa de Santa Eulalia* leave town past taxi rank and turn left at the central crossroads down the N-525 past *café Lago* and turn left **[0.3 km]** (sign Castro de Toiriz) and imm. right along path parallel to the main road with which we play hide and seek on shady paths through the historical nucleus of **Foxo de Deza [1.0** km] *[F.] Botica* (right). Some of the buildings dating back to the 16th century have ancient carvings. We continue out of the hamlet back to the main road and turn left by the Nudesa factory down into the parish of **Margarida** *Centro Cultural* **[1.1** km] *[F.]* (left) shortly afterwards veer off right onto path through woodland emerging onto asphalt road where we have an **option [1.0** km]. The waymarked route turns left and imm. right back onto path or *[Detour right: +200m •H***Eco Rural Nos x6* €60-70 ℂ 928 561 258 **Riocalvo** www.ecohotelnos.com]*. Continue along path past access to Muiño de Covián to bridge over the **río Toxa [1.1** km]. Continue under rail, over AP-53 and onto the **N-525 [2.2** km] for a slog up the main road past the taxi rank and Hotel Rey to the centre of **Bandeira [0.5** km].

7.2 km **Bandeira** Meson Bandeira & Hotel Victorino adj. Hotel Rey opposite the road to the albergue; all conveniently located within 200m. The town has good facilities and a population of 1,000. **Lodging**: •*Hs* **Conde Rey** *x15* €25-35 ℂ 986 585 861 www.hostalconderey.com adj. •*H** **Victorino** *x12* €30-45 ℂ 986 585 330 directly on the N-525. ●*Alb.* **Bandeira** *Mun. [36÷2]* €8 ℂ 670 502 356 modern hostel on rua Louras/c/Agro do Balo adj. *Dia% supermercado*. Leave town on the N-525 and veer **right [0.3** km] onto secondary road relieved by short stretch of path onto country lane into **Dornelas [4.6** km].

4.9 km **Dornelas** ●*Alb.* **Casa Leiras** *Priv. [10÷1]* €12 ℂ 620 483 603 where Andreas provides pilgrim lodging and meals. Continue through the hamlet past *Igrexa de San Martiño*. We now have a 2 kilometre stretch of path through woodland to Crossroads at **Carballeira**. *[Detour +1.2 km <left N-525*: turn down track at side of Rey Iglesias (materiales de construcción Ferretería) and left again on N-525 (imm. right Salon de Te O Peregrino! Casa Márquez and Rst. Emigrante) and continue for only 100m and cross over [!] and follow sign for Lomil and Botica to •H***Casa da Botica x8* €25+ ℂ 677 838 858 www.casadabotica.com *Os Casares]*.

5.0 km **Carballeira** *Cruce* ▲ *[Detour right>* alt. road to **San Miguel de Castro** *Taberna do Seixo & Miradoiro do Alto do Castro*. *Detour <left +0.3 km Meson O Peixeiro +2.5 km* **Oca de Arriba** *Rst.•H***América *x54* €36-46 ℂ 986 587 450 www.hotelrestauranteamerica.com *on N-525 (incl.700m along the busy main road... or take a taxi]*. ▲ Keep s/o over crossroads past *[F.] dos Carballiños* (left) through **Castro** (no facilities). The road now descends sharply down to the río Ulla where we enter town over the original road bridge **Ponte Ulla** *abaixo* **[2.8** km] (N-525 bridge left). *Bar Rios* popular pilgrim stop with restaurant overlooking the river (see photo next page) also rooms •*Hs* **Ríos** *x4* €12+ Hilda ℂ 981 512 305. Adjacent is a pilgrim information office *Información de Peregrino* in the old Casa Rectoral opp. *Iglesia de Santa María Magdalena* and •*P** **Juanito** *x5* €15-25 ℂ 981 512 619 quiet rooms. We now have a climb up to the main road and up the steps to the main centre of activity.

3.3 km **Ponte Ulla** *N-525 arriba*
●*Alb.+Rst.* **O Cruceiro da Ulla** *Priv.*
[18÷8!] €12 +6 €20-35 © 981 512
099 *www.ocruceiro.es* c/Vista Alegre
adj. Motor service station with *Dia%*
supermarket opposite. *[Additional*
facilities and lodging available in
Eiravedra **Santa Cruz de Ribadulla**
1.3 km further on *(400m* **off** *route).*
•*Pr** **Victoria** *x10* €30+ © 981 512

216 *www.hostalresidenciavictoria.es*]. The albergue in **Outeiro** is **4.3** km
further on, a good option if you intend to visit the Pico Santo which is close
by (see next stage). Note that there are no other facilities, restaurants or bars
in Outeiro so eat or buy food in Ponte Ulla before proceeding).

REFLECTIONS:

5 PONTE ULLA – SANTIAGO
21.7 km – Santiago

⁝⁝⁝⁝⁝⁝⁝	--- ---	6.8	--- ---	*31%*
▬▬▬	--- ---	12.6	--- ---	*58%*
▬▬▬	--- ---	<u>2.3</u>	--- ---	*11%*
Total km	--- ---	**21.7 km (13.5 ml)**		

◣ *equiv.* Ascent 1,450m (+7.2 =**28.9** km)
Alto.m ▲ Lestedo 340m (1,115 ft)
< Ⓐ Ⓗ > Outeiro **4.3** km – A Gandara **10.8**

It is good to have an end to journey towards. But it is the journey that matters in the end. Ursula Le Guin.

❏ **Mystical Path:** Where did we begin and where will we end? Sevilla to Santiago is around 1,000 kilometres –100 from Ourense. What did we set out to find? The new is found when we have the courage to let go the old. Endings are often accompanied by sadness – the end of a holiday, death of a loved one. However, a purpose of pilgrimage is to grasp new beginnings, to see beyond the physical to the metaphysical, to move beyond the mundane to the numinous. *Rumi* reminds us, *What we call salvation belongs to the time before death. If we don't break our ropes while we are alive, do we think ghosts will do it after?...*

❏ **Practical Path:** An undulating day as we wend our way around 5 river valleys. Facilities en route are limited although there are several cafés (signposted) just off route – bring water and energy snacks. If time allows, or your interest is piqued, a visit to the Pico Santo with its mythical links to the Santiago story is worth considering (see next page). We cross the busy N-525 several times as we approach the city so take extra care of the traffic and vigilance for the waymarks that blur with other signs competing for our attention.

0.0 km **Ponte Ulla** *arriba* keep s/o past alb. O Cruceiro onto N-525 *[!]* for ½ km along before taking side road left to pass back over N-525 onto a track and under local rail **tunnel [1.5 km]** and turn right at next **crossroads ✚ [0.4 km]** *[Detour left + 400m to •Pr*** **Victoria x10 €40 © 981 512 216 Eiravedra Santa Cruz de Ribadulla].* ✚ We now enter a peaceful uphill stretch of dense

PONTE ULLA – SANTIAGO – 21.7 km

minoGuides.com
S.Susana
Alameda
Santiago Catedral 1.5
SANTIAGO
AP-9
3.7 Puente río Sar
S.María do Sar XII
río Ulla
Monte Viso
Rozas
AC-261
300m
Los Cruces +50m
5.7 Santa Lucia Capela
N-525
S.Lucia
200m
local
AVE
300m
AP-59
AP-53
rego Marrozos
SUSANA
Fogar Do Abó +200m
Reina Lupa
Bar Rosende
Opción Albergue 3.3
A GANDARA
río Saramo
AC-920
200m
W
Sunset
S
Sunrise
E
BOQUEIXÓN
Rubial
LESTEDO
Casa de Casal + 0.3 km
Cruce 3.2
Cruceiro Lestedo
Vía da Prata + 0.6 km
490m
340m
Pico Sacro
Ermita
300m
400m
N-525
Outeiro
4.3 Outeiro Albergue
Ermita Santiago
Fuente Santiago
VEDRA
+ 0.9 km Pazo de Galegos
local
AC-240
300m
+ 0.5 km Pazo de Galegos
AVE
AC-241
200m
río Ulla
100m
O Cruceiro
Ponte Ulla Arriba 0.0
PONTE ULLA
río Ulla
70m

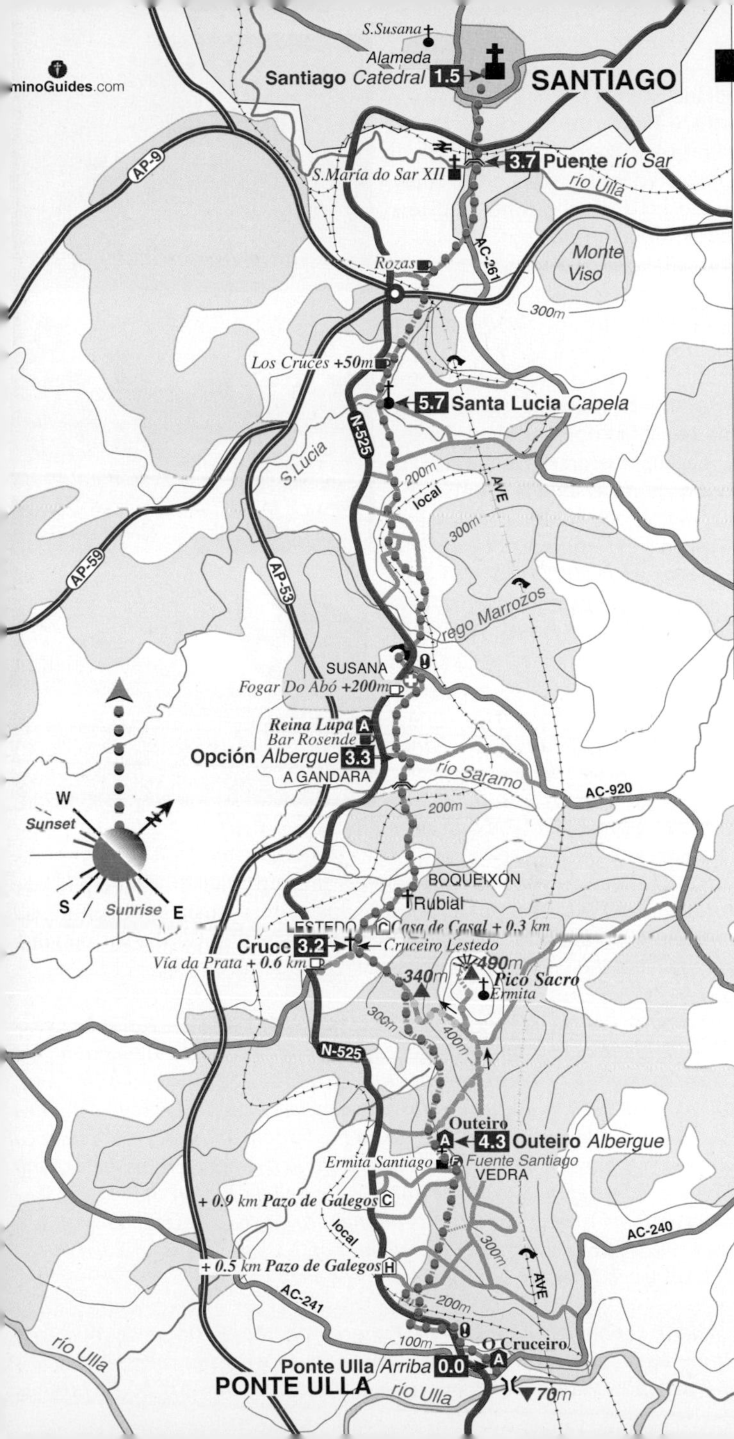

woodland to emerge at the emblematic **Ermita** *y* **Fonte de Santiago** *XVIIc.* **[2.2** km] (see photo>) in the parish of San Pedro Vilanova (Concello Vedra). Keep s/o between the fonte and rear of the hermitage into gravel track to Outeiro albergue **[0.2** km]**.

4.3 km **Albergue** ●*Alb.***Outeiro** *Xunta. [32÷2]* €8 ℂ 689 352 875. Peaceful location overlooking the surrounding countryside. Note there are no other facilities or shops in the area. The next nearest restaurant *Via da Prata* is in Lestedo 3.2 km and a further 600m off route – a possible breakast stop? *[Detour + 0.9 km •Pazo de Galegos x9 €60-€90 ℂ 981 512 217* www.pazodegalegos.com *Lugar de Galegos, 6. San Pedro. Ancestral home of famous Galician writer Don Antonio Lopez Ferreiro canon of the cathedral of Santiago. Now home to vineyards producing local wines incl. Mencía, Albariño and Godello. Directions: At Ermita Santiago turn down road and just before N-525 turn left - signposted].*

The mythical Sacred Peak *Pico Sacro 490m* rises up behind the albergue (see photo above) and is best approached from this point. A steep uphill climb, all by quiet asphalt road, is rewarded with wonderful views over the surrounding countryside and the spires of Santiago cathedral in the far distance.

*[**Directions:** From the albergue take first turn right [0.1 km] and keep s/o uphill to T-junction [1.2 km] turn left and left again at next T-junction [0.4 km]. Turn up right [0.1 km] to access road ▲ to Pico Santo chapel [0.6 km]. Uphill distance **2.4** km. Return to the waymarked route in Lestedo (no need to return to the albergue) as follows: ▲ at the bottom of the access road turn down right (we arrived by the level road to the left) and keep on the asphalt road ignoring any enticing gravel tracks right or left. Rejoin the waymarked route by Attelier Carmen Pichel and continue s/o down to Lestedo crossroads. Return distance **2.7** km for a combined **total of 5.1** km -versus- **3.2** km on the direct level track from the albergue.*

Pico Sacro competes with Castro Lupario on the Portuguese Way and Finisterre as locations for the legendary battle of wills between Sant Iago's faithful disciples who were trying to find a place to bury his body. Little is written about this legend and yet it is the very reason you are here! All 80,000 kilometres of waymarked caminos lead to his tomb. Without the tomb there would me no camino de Santiago with 3 million visitors a year. You are one of the ½ million who will arrive on foot. Whether or not you are religious or walk the path for a spiritual purpose you are here, at this very spot, because of this legend.

Let's recap: St. James came to this part of Iberia to preach his master's message of unconditional love. He returns to the Holy Land and is himself martyred and his disciples are called to bring his body back to the place of his early ministry. They land in Padron (Iria Flavia) and seek a place to bury his remains but are constantly 'moved on' as the lands St. James ministered to have not (yet) embraced Christianity or its message. The cortège eventually seek permission of the pagan Queen Lupa but she tricks them and sends them to a place (Pico Sacro) to harness some docile oxen who turn out to be wild bulls with the intention they all be killed and their bodies lost. However, the bulls are instantly tamed and Queen Lupa converted... and all live happily ever after?

To proceed directly to Lestedo from the albergue keep s/o along the wide gravel track over several cross roads and tracks to high point for this stage *Alto 340m* by house *Attelier Carmen Pichel*. We turn down left on asphalt road (Pico Santo up right 490m) past sports pavilion *pabellón Lestedo* (right) to crossroads.

3.2 km **Cruce Lestedo** *cruceiro [Detour left 600m (1.2 km return!) Rst. Vía da Prata © 981 502 102 opens 7 a.m.?]*. Turn down right and left at next **crossroads [0.3 km]** *[Detour s/o + 350m •CR* **Casa de Casal** *x9 €65 © 981 503 227 www.casadecasal.com Lugar de Cuchosenande, Lestedo (Boqueixón) signposted]*. The way continues by a series of quiet lanes partly shaded with woodland to crossroads **Rubial [1.0 km]** Pazo (right) with cruceiro, statue of Santiago in niche and plaque *[stating that the wild (now tamed) bulls pulling Santiago's hearse rested at this spot along with disciples S. Teodoro & S. Antastaso on their way to Libredon – now Santiago)]*. We turn down left past Villa Irene and continue to zigzag along country lanes – well waymarked to cross over **rego Marrozos [1.5 km]** turn left to **option point [0.5 km]** just before the N-525 with bar clearly visible ahead.

3.3 km **Option** *N-525 + 100m* ●*Alb.* **Reina Lupa** *Priv. [14÷2] €14 x2 €40 + adj.* *Bar Rosende © 981 511 803 www.alberguereinalupa.com* directly on the N-525 (see photo>). If you take this option return to the option point and head up to T-junction in woodland where we have another option to take the track +200m to *Fogar Do Abó* also on the N-525. Turn right down to

N-525 and cross over, pedestrian crossing by ✚ *Farmacia* onto side road that curves around to pass under the N-525 and then over the rego Marrozos and under rail line onto a series of quiet lane-ways to:

5.7 km **Capela** *Santa Lucia* situated alongside the rego Santa Lucia by a shaded grove. Keep s/o past wayside cross along the camino Real through the hamlet of Piñeiro to **crossroads [0.7 km]**. *[Detour 50m left (signposted) to café Los Cruces]*. Keep s/o at crossroads onto peaceful woodland path under motorway to shaded picnic area *Parque de Angrois [F.]* **[1.1 km]** overlooking the junction of the motorway and AVE and local rail lines.

[✚ This is the point at which the train carrying pilgrims to Santiago to celebrate St. James Day crashed on the 24 July 2013 killing 79 pilgrims in Spain's worst rail disaster. Celebrations around the world were cancelled the following day as a mark of respect]. Continue over the rail line, which remains as an informal memorial site *A Grandeira*, past *café Rozas* up along the camino Real de Angrois to high point with ancient *cruceiro* **[1.0 km]** (right). Cross over the main road **[!]** onto the quaint cobbled lane *rúa do Sar* where a lovely view of Santiago cathedral opens up, the 'Monte do Gozo' of our route. We continue down to cross the bridge over the **río Sar [0.9 km]**.

3.7 km **Ponte río Sar** a *pasarela* adjoins the original road bridge and we come to the historic collegiate church *Igrexa Santa Maria Real do Sar XIIc.* over to our left (100m). Interesting Romanesque building that began to sink into the river Sar and so the enormous flying buttresses were added in the 18th century to prevent its collapse. It was the first
Augustinian house in Galicia. The adj. priory is a Religious Art Museum *Museo Da Colexiata Do Sar*. Continue up and under the ring road SC-20 past •H*** **San Nicolás** €60 ℂ 981 587 554 *www.casa-sannicolas.com* Rúa de Sar, 1 with delightful courtyard restaurant *O Sendeiro*. Towards the top of the street we pass •Hs** **La Carballinesa** €40+ ℂ 981 586 261 Rúa do Patio de Madres, 14 adj. •**Casa Douro** from €29 ℂ 630 560 602.

Cross the busy Rúa da Fonte de San Antonio **[!]** and up and under the historic *Arco de Mazarelos* and s/o through Prazas Mazarelos, Universidade, Fonte Seca into r/ Castro and turn down left by ✚ *Farmacia Martinez* into r/ de Xelmírez passing r/ Nova (left) with private pilgrim services incl. backpack storage named simply ● *Pilgrim* at r/ Nova 7 ℂ +44 20 396 638 00 *www.info@pilgrim.es* open daily 9:30 – 20:00 / Sat. 9:30 –18:30 closed Sun. Continue for 100m to:

1.5 km **Catedral de Santiago** *Praza das Praterías*. Take a few moments to just arrive. Pilgrims coming from Ourense and the Portuguese routes traditionally enter the cathedral by the south door off *Praza das Praterías*. This is the oldest and, arguably, the most beautiful doorway to the Cathedral dating back to the 11th century (1078). The magnificent stone carvings surrounding this portal

show hardly a hint of the intervening 900 years. St. James is represented in the centre between 2 cypress tress next to Christ. Many pilgrims prefer to go direct to the main square *Praza do Obradoiro* with its throng of pilgrims coming from the camino Francés and interconnecting routes to enter through the west door with the Portico do Gloria. Cathedral open daily 09:00 – 20:00.
Pilgrim Mass at Noon each day. *[Check times: www.catedraldesantiago.es].* Mass in English celebrated at 09:30 in the lovely chapel in the Pilgrims office complex. **Note:** backpacks are no longer allowed in the cathedral so you need to either **[a]** check in to your accommodation or **[b]** go straight to the pilgrim office and welcome centre now located a further 500m on the far side of the cathedral (see city map) or **[c]** check your backpack into one of several left luggage facilities. The nearest is ● *Pilgrim* (see previous page).

Whichever square you end your journey we each will have different emotions after weeks of solitary walking with its physical, emotional and spiritual challenges. Entering the cathedral can bring tears of joy… or disappointment. Gratitude for our safe arrival is a universally appropriate response. However, if you are overwhelmed by the crowds why not return later when you might feel more composed and the cathedral is, perhaps, quieter.

Praza das Praterías Cathedral South Door

Whether now or later you might like to follow the time-worn pilgrim ritual as follows *(ongoing cathedral renovations and new regulations allowing)*:

Ⓐ Stand before the Tree of Jesse, the central column of Master Mateo's masterpiece: the Entrance of Glory *Pórtico da Gloria*. Millions of pilgrims, over the millennia, have worn down the solid marble as they placed their hands there as a mark of gratitude for their safe arrival (a barrier was placed here in 2007 to prevent further wear) but we can breathe in the beauty of this inner portico fashioned by Mateo in the 12th century (the outer porch was added in 1750). The Bible and its main characters come alive in this remarkable marble façade. The central column has Christ in Glory, flanked by the apostles and, directly underneath, St. James sits as intercessor between Christ and the pilgrim.

Ⓑ On the other side pilgrims of yore would touch their brow to that of Maestro Mateo, whose kneeling figure is carved into the back of the central column (facing the altar) and receive some of his artistic genius in the ritual known as the head-butting saint *santo dos croques*. **Ⓒ** Go to the High Altar (right hand side) to ascend the stairs and hug the Apostle. Perhaps lay your forehead on his broad shoulders and say what you came here to say. Whatever your motivation and beliefs you have arrived here in one piece because, on some level, of the call of St. James. **Ⓓ** Proceed down the steps to the far side to the crypt and the reliquary chapel under the altar. Here you can kneel before the casket containing the relics of the great Saint and offer your prayer.

The swinging of the giant incense burner ***Botafumeiro*** often takes place at the 12 noon pilgrim mass. *[**Note:** check: www.catedraldesantiago.es]*. It was originally used to fumigate the sweaty (and possibly disease ridden) pilgrims. Requiring half a dozen assistants *Tiraboleiros* it became a rare occurrence, but is used increasingly during mass these days. It is certainly a very moving and unique experience despite the constant sound and flash of cameras.

Four squares surround the cathedral:

■ **Praza do Obradoiro**. The 'golden' square of Santiago is usually thronged with pilgrims and tourists admiring the dramatic west facing façade of the Cathedral, universal symbol of Santiago, with St. James looking down on all the activity from his niche in the central tower. This provides the main entrance to the Cathedral and the Portico de Gloria. To the right of the steps is the discrete entrance to the museum. A combined ticket will provide access to all rooms including

the crypt and the cloisters and also to the 12th century palace of one of Santiago's most famous individuals and first archbishop, Gelmírez *Pazo de Xelmírez* situated on the (left). In this square we also find the beautiful Renaissance façade of the Parador named after Ferdinand and Isabel *Hostal dos Reis Católicos* on whose orders it was built in 1492 as a pilgrim hospice. Opposite the Cathedral is the more austere neoclassical town hall *Pazo de Raxoi XVIIIc.* with its solid arcade and seat of the City Council and various Galician government offices. Finally, making up the fourth side of the square is the gable end of the *Colegio de S. Jerónimo* part of the university. Moving anti-clockwise around the cathedral – turn up into Rúa de Fonseca to:

■ **Praza das Praterías**. The most intimate of the squares with its lovely centrepiece, an ornate statue of four horses leaping out of the water and built in 1759. On the corner of Rúa do Vilar we find the Dean's House *Casa do Deán* the much loved original pilgrim office. Along the walls of the Cathedral itself are the silversmith's *plateros* that give the square its name

(see photo> of cathedral silhouetted in silversmith window *joyeria plateria*).

Up the steep flight of steps we come to the magnificent southern door to the Cathedral, the oldest extant doorway and traditionally the entrance also used by pilgrims coming from Portugal. The quality of the carvings and their arrangement is remarkable and amongst the many sculptured figures is the one of St. James between two cypress trees (see photo previous page). Continuing around to the right we come to:

■ **Praza da Quintana.** This wide square is identified by the broad sweep of steps separating the lower part *Quintana Muerto (of the dead as it was formerly a cemetery)* from the upper *Quintana Vivos*. Opp. the Cathedral is the wall of *San Paio de Antealtares* (with museum of sacred art). The square provides the eastern entrance to the Cathedral via the Holy Door *Porta Santa* only opened during Holy Years (2027 follows the 2021 Jubilee). To the left is the entrance to the Cathedral gift shop selling guidebooks with details of the Cathedral's many chapels and their interesting carvings and statuary and the priceless artefacts and treasures in the museum. At dusk we might see the 'hidden' pilgrim shadow *el Peregrino Escondido* that some say is Santiago himself! Finally, we head up the broad flight of steps around the corner and back into:

■ **Praza da Inmaculada** the north facing Azabachería façade with the least well-known doorway and the only one that *descends* to enter the Cathedral. It has the most weathered aspect, with moss and lichen covering its bleak exterior. Opposite the cathedral is the imposing southern edifice of *San Martiño Pinario* which gets any available sun and attracts street artists (see photo>). The archbishop's arch *Arco Arzobispal* brings us back to the Praza do Obradoiro.

The **Pilgrim Office** *Oficina del Peregrino* © 981 568 846 rua Carretas *below the parador* Open daily Easter to 31st Oct. 08.00-20.00 / Winter 1st Nov.-Easter 10.00-19.00 (excluding Christmas & New Years day). *oficinadelperegrino@catedraldesantiago.es* The new office has tight security procedure (expect lengthy delays). It lacks the informal atmosphere of the former office in rua Vilar but retains its team of *Amigos*. Providing you have fulfilled the criteria of a bona fide pilgrim and walked at least the last 100 km (200 km on bike or horseback) for religious/spiritual reasons and collected 2 stamps per day on your *credencial* you will be awarded the *Compostela* which may entitle you to certain privileges such as reduced entry fees to museums and a free meal at the Parador! If you do not fulfil the criteria you may still be able to obtain a ***certificado*** (€3) which is essentially a certificate of distance travelled. The welcoming Companions meet in a room behind the adjoining pilgrim chapel (see below).

•**Camino Companions** meet in pilgrim office *chapel* 09:00 & 14:30 May– Oct for reflection and integration (see Facebook for updates) + Prayer / Taizé at 17:00. •**The Camino Chaplaincy** offers Mass in English daily at 10:30 & Sunday 09:00 May–Oct. in the cathedral *Capela N.S. de la Soledad*. •**Pilgrim House** rua Nova 19 also offers a place of welcome and reflection 11:00–20:00 (closed Wed & Sun) under the care of Terra Nova USA.

Lodging in the city listed overleaf. Albergues located to the east of the city on the ***camino Francés*** as follows: ∎ **Monte del Gozo:** *Alb.* ❶ **Benvido** *Xunta.* *[770÷120]* €12-16 *+100* €35 dbl. ©881 255 386 *www.benvidomontedogozo.com* Refurbished 2019 with 970 beds in separate blockhouses (4-8 beds in each room) *cantina* on the main plaza. ∎ *San Lázaro:* Behind *Museo Pedagóxico* ❷ **San Lázaro** *Xunta.[80÷6]* €10 (€7 for 2nd & 3rd nights) © 981 571 488 all facilities opens 9 a.m. ❸ **Fin del Camino** *Asoc.[112÷8]* €10 c/Moscova & corner r/Roma modern building with all facilities. ∎ **Rúa do Valiño** *['below' the park (steep steps left)]:* ❹ **Acuario** *Priv.*[60÷7]* €10-12 © 981 575 438 r/ Estocolmo 2. Keep s/o to Nº3 ❺ **Santo Santiago** *Priv.[40÷3]* €10-12 © 657 402 403. adj. •*H* S.Lazaro €35+ © 981 584 344. Pass viewpoint into ∎ **Rúa das Fontiñas** Nº65 ❻ **Monterey** *Priv.[36÷1]* €10-14 © 655 484 299 s/o into ∎ **Rúa da Fonte dos Conchciros** Nº13 (corner of r/Altiboia) ❼ **La credencial** *Priv.[36÷3]* €10-14 © 639 966 704. ❽ **Nº2c SCQ** *Priv.[24÷4]* €14-16 © 622 037 300. Nº2a ❾ **Sixtos no Caminho** *Priv.[40÷1]* €15-20 © 881 024 195 *www.alberguesixtos.com* (corner of Av.Lugo).

● **Turismo** *Centro*: r/ Vilar 63 © 981 555 129 *www.santiagoturismo.com*
May-Oct: 09:00-19.00 (winter 17:00) ● **Tur Galicia** Praza de Mazarelos
10:00 / 17:00 ● **Pilgrim Services** Rúa Nova 7 (adj. catedral) © 912 913 756
left luggage €3. ●**Laundromat SC18** 09:00-22:00 Rúa San Clemente 18.

■*Albergues: €10-€20* (depending on season / beds per dormitory) ❶–❾ *(camino
Francés –see prev. page).* ■ **Rúa Concheiros Nº48** ❿ **El Viejo Quijote** *Priv.
[20÷2]* © 881 088 789. **Nº36** ⓫ **La Estrella** *Priv.[24÷6]* © 617 882 529. **Nº10**
⓬ **Porta Real** *Priv.[20÷6]* © 633 610 114. ■ **Belvís +500m** ⓭ **Seminario
Menor** *Conv.[173÷12]+81* © 881 031
768 *www.alberguesdelcamino.com* Av.
Quiroga Palacios *(see photo>).* ■ **c/**

S.Clara ⓮ **La Salle** *Priv.[84÷14]* ©
981 585 667 ■ **c/ Basquiños Nº45** ⓯
Basquiños *Priv.[8÷1]* © 661 894 536
Nº67 ⓰ **Meiga Backpackers** *Priv.
[28÷5]* © 981 570 846.

■ **Centro Histórico:** ⓱ **O Fogar de Teodomiro** *Priv.[20÷5]+* © 981 582 920
Plaza de Algalia de Arriba 3. ⓲ **The Last Stamp** *Priv.[62÷10]* © 981 563 525
r/ Preguntorio 10. ⓳ **Azabache** *Priv.[20÷5]* © 981 071 254 c/Azabachería
15. ⓴ **Km.0** *Priv.[50÷10]* (€ 18-26) © 881 974 992 *www.santiagokm0.es* r/
Carretas 11 (new renovation by pilgrim office) ㉑ **Blanco** *Priv.[20÷2]+ +€35-
55* © 881 976 850 r/ Galeras 30. ㉒ **Mundoalbergue** *Priv.[34÷1]* © 981 588
625 c/ San Clemente 26. ㉓ *Roots & Boots (closed temp.) Priv.[48÷6]* © 699
631 594 r/Campo Cruceiro do Galo.* ■ *Otros:* ㉔ **La Estación** *Priv.[24÷2]* ©
981 594 624 r/ Xoana Nogueira 14 (adj. rail station **+2.9** km). ㉕ **Compostela
Inn** *Priv.[120÷30]+* © 981 819 030 off *AC-841 (adj. H Congreso +6.0 km).*

■ *Hoteles €30–60:* •*Hs* **Santiago** © 608 865 895 r/Senra 11. •*Hs* **Moure**
© 981 583 637 r/dos Loureiros. •*H* **Fonte S. Roque** © 981 554 447 r/do
Hospitalilo 8. •*Hs* **Estrela** © 981 576 924 Plaza de San Martín Pinario 5.
•*Hs* **San Martín Pinario** *x127* © 981 560 282 *www.hsanmartinpinario.com*
Praza da Inmaculada. •**Pico Sacro** r/San Francisco 22 © 981 584 466. •*H***
Montes © 981 574 458 *www.hotelmontes.es* r/ Raíña 11. **Rúa Fonseca Nº1** •*P*
Fonseca © 603 259 337. **Nº5** •*Hs* **Libredon** 981 576 520 & •*P* **Barbantes /
Celsa** ©981 583 271 on r/ Franco 3. **Rúa Vilar Nº8** •*H******Rua Vilar** © 981 519
858. **Nº17** •*H*****Airas Nunes** © 981 569 350. **Nº65** •*Hs*****Suso** © 981 586 611
www.hostalsuso.com. **Nº76** •*Hs* **Santo Grial** © 629 515 961. •**A Nosa Casa**
© 981 585 926 r/ Entremuralles 9 adj. •*Hs* **Mapoula** © 981 580 124. •*Hs*
Alameda © 981 588 100 San Clemente 32. ■ *€60–90:* •*H* **A Casa Peregrino**
© 981 573 931 c/ Azabachería. •**Entrecercas** © 981 571 151 r/Entrecercas.
Porta de Pena Nº17 •*H* **Costa Vella** © 981 569 530 (+ Jardín) **Nº5** •*P* **Casa
Felisa** © 981 582 602 (+Jardín). •**MV Algalia** © 981 558 111 Praza Algalia
de Arriba 5. •*H******Pazo De Altamira** © 981 558 542 r/ Altamira, 18. ■ *€100+*
•*H**** **San Francisco** Campillo de San Francisco © 981 581 634. •*H**** **Hostal
de los Reyes Católicos** Plaza Obradoiro © 981 582 200.

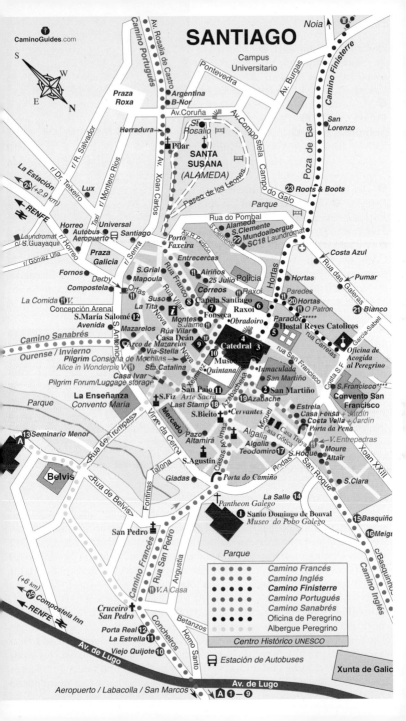

❑ *Centro Histórico*: ❶ Convento de Santo Domingo Bonaval *XIIIc. (panteón de Castelao, Rosalía de Castro y museo do Pobo Galego).* ❷ Mosteiro *y museo* de San Martín Pinario *XVIc.* ❸ Pazo *y museo* de Xelmirez *XIIc.* ❹ Catedral *XIIc. – XVIIIc. Portica de Gloria, claustro, museo e tesouro (photo> altar above crypt housing the relics of St. James).* ❺ Hostal dos Reis Católicos *XVc. Parador* ❻ Pazo de Raxoi *XVIIIc. Presendencia da Xunta* ❼ Colexio de Fonseca *XVIc. universidade y claustro* ❽ Capela *y Fonte* de Santiago ❾ Casa do Deán *XVIIIc. Oficina do*

Peregrino (original). ❿ Casa Canónica *museo Peregrinaciónes.* ⓫ Mosteiro de San Paio de Antealtares *XVc. Museo de Arte Sacra.* ⓬ Igrexa de Santa Maria Salomé *XIIc.*

Santiago is a wonderful destination, full of vibrancy and colour. Pilgrims, musicians, dancers, tourists... all come and add to the life and soul of this fabled city. Stay awhile and visit her museums and markets. Soak up some of her culture or relax in the delightful shaded park *Alameda* and stroll up the avenue of the Lions *Paseo dos Leónes* to the statue of Rosalia de Castro and look out west over her belovéd Galicia and... *Finis terrae.* Have you time to walk the camino to the end of the

world? See a Pilgrim's Guide to Finisterre for the rich legends that surround this mythical headland that is a central part of the caminos de Santiago story. A fire-pit at the base of a cross invites the burning of an outworn item of clothing and the donning of a new one to symbolise spiritual renewal. It supersedes a similar tradition at the Cruz dos Ferrapos on the cathedral rooftop (still viewable as part of the guided rooftop tour).

Returning Home: Galicia has 3 airports: Santiago, A Coruña and Vigo. Also check flights from Porto and note there are regular bus services direct to Porto Airport *alsa.com* with journey time around 4 hours (via Vigo and Tuy) cost ±€25 also rail with *renfe.com* There is a twice daily bus service from Santiago direct to Madrid airport with a journey time of 8 hours 45 minutes cost ±€50. Onward suggestions by air, rail, bus and car to all destinations check *www.rome2rio.com*

REFLECTIONS: *How can I mark the end of this journey as part of a discovery of a Self that I never knew I had. And what awaits me as I take my next steps into a future quite unlike the past.*

_____
_____
_____
_____
_____
_____
_____
_____
_____
_____
_____
_____
_____
_____
_____
_____
_____
_____
_____
_____
_____
_____

The breeze at dawn has something to tell you. Don't go back to sleep. Rumi.

Camino Invierno
Ponferrada – A laxe – Santiago

*A Practical & Mystical Manual
for the Modern-day Pilgrim*

John Brierley

PONFERRADA: Capital of El Bierzo with a population of 65,000. Whether commencing your journey here or you have decided to branch off along the camino Invierno from the camino Francés, take time to explore the old town. Most of the historic sites are neatly condensed into the old medieval city that occupies the high ground around the castle. The town is named after the iron bridge *Pons Ferrata* built over the río Sil. The bridge gives the city its name and the reason for the sprawling modern suburbs that support a strong industrial base built on the back of the coal and iron reserves that have been mined in this area from medieval times. The original bridge was reinforced with iron as far back as the 11th century. The former power station has been converted to a museum *Museo de la Energía* (10:30-14:30) with *Café* and lies a 1.4 km detour along the río Sil via the peaceful *Parque de la Concordia*. The camino Invierno starts at the cross with Santiago image adj. to albergue Guiana to leave town by the medieval Puente Mascarón over the río Boeza.

❏ **Tourist Office** *Turismo*: © 987 424 236 *www.ponferrada.org/turismo/es* c/ Gil y carrasco (castle entrance) daily 10:00-14:00 Mon-Sat: 16:30-20:30.

❏ **Lodging:** *Alb.*❶ **San Nicolás de Flüe** *Mun.[180÷7]* €-donativo © 987 413 381 *www.sannicolasdeflue.com* c/de la Loma in grounds of the convento del Carmen (off Av. del Castillo) purpose-built hostel with patio and garden area (see photo>). Evening prayers offered.

*Alb.*❷ **Alea** *Priv.[18÷4]* €11 menú €8 *V.option* © 987 404 133 m: 660 416 251 *www.alberguealea.com* c/Teleno, 33 modern suburbs with quiet garden patio. *Alb.*❸ **Guiana** *Priv.[90÷14]* €12 +6 €50 © 987 409 327 *www. albergueguiana.com* Av del Castillo, 112 with all modern facilities and basic starting point for the camino Invierno (guidebooks available here). See photo>

❏ *Hoteles Centro: Av del Castillo:* @*Nº84 Rst.*•*Hs*****Rabel** *x10* €38-45 © 987 417 176 *www.hostalrabel.com* @*Nº115 Rst.*•*H******El Castillo** *x40* €39-55 ©987 456 227 *https://hotelelcastilloponferrada.h-rez.com* •*Hs*** **Virgen de la Encina** *x13* €35-50 © 987 409 632 c/Comendador *www.hostallaencina. net* •*H*****Alda Los Templarios** *x18* €37-45 © 987 625 146 c/ FlórezOsorio,3. •*H******Aroi Bierzo Plaza** *x30* €50+ © 987 409 001 *www.aroihotelescom* Plaza del Ayuntamiento.

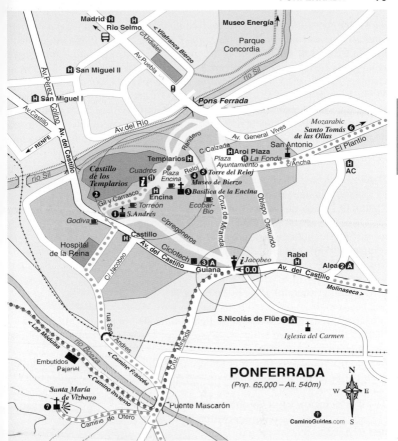

Other side of rio Sil: •*Hs*** **Río Selmo** *x17* €35-45 ℰ 987 402 665 <u>www.</u><u>hostalrioselmo.com</u> c/Río Selmo,22. •*H**** **Madrid** ℰ 987 411 550 Av. Puebla,44. •*Hs* **San Miguel II** ℰ 987 426 700 *x15* €30-45 c/Juan de Lama,14.

❏ *Restaurants:* wide selection includes: *Las Cuadras* c/ Gil y carrasco (by castle). *La Fonda* plaza Ayuntamiento (first floor). *Café Godiva* opp. Castle (evening sun). ❏ *Ciclotech* + ponchos etc. Av. Castillo 128 ℰ 987 032 394.

❏ **Monumentos Historicos:** ❶ *Iglesia San Andrés XVII*c. Baroque Church with statue *Cristo del Castillo* linking it to the Knights Templars. ❷ *Castillo de los Templarios* magnificent XIIthc Templar castle recently reopened after extensive renovations so we can explore its interior and revel in its romantic past. A modern exhibition centre has been added which currently displays replicas of Templar and other religious texts in the *Templum Libri* accessed by lift! *[Ponferrada came under the protectorate of the Templar Order by decree of King Fernando II in 1178. Their official presence here was short lived as* *the Order was outlawed in 1312 and disbanded by a Church fearful of their increasing power and esoteric traditions].* Off the central Plaza Virgen de la Encina we find ❸ *Basílica de la Encina* XVIc. *[In bygone days this whole region was covered with evergreen holm oak* encina *and in one such tree a vision of the Virgin appeared elevating this church to Basilica status and the Virgin to patroness of the Bierzo region].* ❹ *Cárcel Real* XVIc. the Royal Prison on c/Reloj worth a visit just for the beautifully restored building now the *Museo del Bierzo* displaying artefacts from the Palaeolithic, Roman and modern eras. ❺ *La Torre del Reloj* XVIc. the Clock Tower leads into the fine Plaza Mayor with its impressive town hall *Ayuntamiento*.

Detour +1.6 km North of the town hall *Ayuntamiento* past Parque del Plantío ❻ **Iglesia de Santo Tomás de las Ollas** *Xc.* Mozarabic church with its distinctive horseshoe arches. The original pilgrim road into the city used to go by here. It is little visited but well worth the trip if you are staying in Ponferrada (helpful lady in house adj. has key). It is connected to the *Xc.* Mozarabic church of **Santiago de Peñalba** located in a mountain hideaway in the Valley of Silence *Valle del Silencio* 20 km south of Ponferrada.

Detour +500m from Puente Mascarón) ❼ **Iglesia de Santa María de Vizbayo** *XI[th]c* Romanesque with view over the city from its hillside site.

The Bierzo region has a unique micro climate and mineral soil composition that produces the respected Bierzo wines. The uniqueness of the terroir adds delightful nuances to the wines of Bierzo and has been described as the wine worlds best kept secret! The *Mencia* grape tends to predominate and is well worth sampling while in its own *Denominación de Origen* D.O. along with the local pork sausages *botillo* locally marinated and served with cabbage and boiled potatoes known as *cachelos*.

Notes / Reflections:

01 PONFERRADA – Las MÉDULAS
Santiago—274.3 km

▦▦▦▦▦	--- ---	15.8	--- ---	55%
▧▧▧▧▧	--- ---	12.5	--- ---	44%
▬▬▬▬	--- ---	0.4	--- ---	1%
Total km		**28.7** km (17.8 ml)		

△ *equiv.* Ascent 1,470m (+7.3 =**36.0** km)
Alto.m ▲ Corantel 825m (2,710 ft)
< Ⓐ Ⓗ > Villavieja **16.8** km Borrones **21.8**
[25.2 km: Carucedo + 0.4 – Orellán + 2.5]

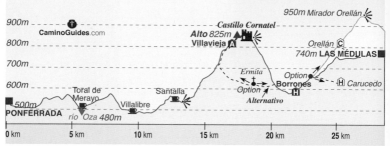

O, Sunlight! The most precious gold to be found on Earth. Roman Payne.

❏ **Mystical Path:** Light illuminates our path and casts shadows where it fails to penetrate. The allegory of Plato's Cave is apt for our time... it's time to awaken to a new reality. The caves of Las Médulas were hewn by those in bondage and designed by those in bondage too – everyone was bound to the Roman coin of the empire. We have to break free from own imprisonment and a consensus reality that no longer holds true. We need a paradigm shift in consciousness to a new sovereignty of thought and values.

❏ **Practical Path:** A Spectacular, if arduous stage, with cumulative ascent of 1,470m (equivalent to extra 7.3 km in effort). Consider stopover at interim lodging (see above). Over ½ this stage is on natural tracks through woodland, mostly chestnut *castaños*. The route follows the river Sil valley (480m) with a wonderful climb up to Villavieja and Castillo Corantel (825m) with a second steep climb to Las Médulas (740m). UNESCO World Heritage Site and stunning landscape – Make time to explore the area (Note: This is a popular tourist site so lodging is in high demand – you may need to book lodging elsewhere). Extensive woodland and north facing slopes of Monte Pajariel provide good shade from sun and wind. There are cafés and water fonts in most of the villages but fill up regularly and bring food for an evening meal if staying at the albergue in Villavieja *(scenic location but no facilities)*.

0.0 km **Ponferrada** *Cruceiro* A natural start point is the Santiago cross in

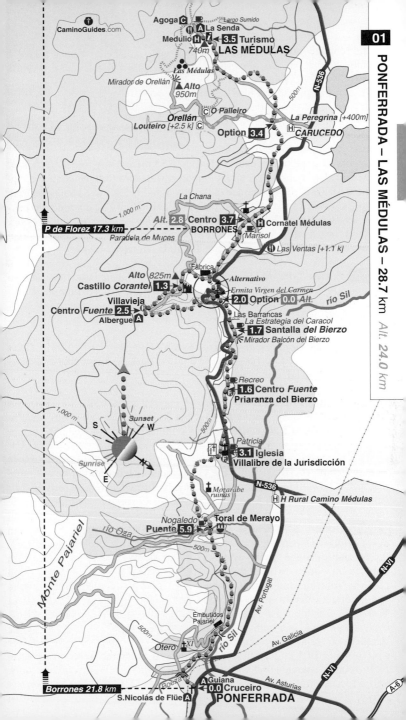

CaminoGuides.com

Agoga **C**

Largo Sumido

A La Senda

Medulio **H** **7** **3.5** Turismo

LAS MÉDULAS

740m

Las Médulas

Mirador de Orellán

▲ **Alto**
950m

Orellán **C** O Palleiro

Louteiro [+2.5 k] **C**

H La Peregrina [+400m]

Option **3.4**

CARUCEDO

N-536

500m

La Chana

Alt. **2.8** Centro **3.7**
BORRONES

H Cornatel Médulas

Paradela de Muces

Marisol

1.000 m

II *Las Ventas [+1.1 k]*

Fábrica

▲ **Alto** *825m*

Castillo *Corantel* **1.3**

Villavieja

Centro *Fuente* **2.5**

Albergue **A**

Alternativo

Ermita Virgen del Carmen

2.0 Option **0.0** *Alt.*

río Sil

Las Barrancas
La Estrategia del Caracol

1.7 Santalla *del Bierzo*

Mirador Balcón del Bierzo

Recreo

1.6 Centro *Fuente*

Priaranza del Bierzo

S

W

Sunset

Sunrise

E

1.000 m

Patricia

3.1 Iglesia

Villalibre de la Jurisdicción

N-536

† *Mozárabe ruinas*

H H Rural Camino Médulas

Nogaledo

Puente **5.9**

Toral de Merayo

río Oza

500m

Monte Pajariel

Embutidos Pajariel

Otero † XI

río Sil

Av. Portugal

Av. Galicia

N-VI

500m

Boeza

A Guiana

0.0 Cruceiro

PONFERRADA

Av. Asturias

A-6

Borrones 21.8 km

S.Nicolás de Flüe **A**

P de Florez 17.3 km

central roundabout of Av. Castillo adj. camino info. kiosk **Jacobeo** (often closed) & •*Alb.* **Guiana** (generally open; caminoguides available here). Head down c/Cruz de Miranda passing first concrete bollard *Mojón* with camino Invierno waymark (see photo). Continue down over railway and medieval stone bridge over **río Boeza [0.5** km] and turn right> *(Iglesia de Santa María de Vizbayo Xc. up left)* along c/Matadero past the confluence of the río Boeza and río Sil (hidden in the woodland below) to pass a pedestrian bridge *pasarela* over the **río Sil [1.2** km] and shortly afterwards we pass Casa del Botillo and Embutidos Pajariel *(chorizo & other traditional pork products from Spain).* At this point the asphalt ends and we start the first long section of delightful forest track into **Toral de Merayo [4.2** km]:

5.9 km **Puente** *Toral de Merayo* over río Oza *bar Puente* into village square *[F.]* and *café Nogaledo.* Turn up into c/ Merayo past *(CR **Miralmonte** © 987 419 475 house only to let)* Iglesia and *sign* for Iglesia Mozarabe (ruins) back onto track veering right at *Finca Costa* and down past cemetery (left) to:

3.1 km **Iglesia** *Villalibre de la Jurisdicción [F.] [café Patricia s/o + 100m off route on main road].* Turn <left at church through village *[F.]* and cross main road N-536 [!] into:

1.6 km **Centro** *Priaranza del Bierzo [F.]* at exit *café el Sitio de mi Recreo (often closed).* Veer up onto path to cross N-536 [!] on dangerous bend at viewpoint *Mirador Balcón del Bierzo.* Continue down into Santalla.

1.7 km **Santalla** *del Bierzo* Café Caracol 'the snail' © 606 141 820 Rosa & Lidia welcome at c/Reguerai in the village centre (a bed might be available if in need – awaiting licence) *(note: CR **Las Barrancas** house only to let).* Continue onto quiet path to option point **Virgin Carmen hermitage**:

2.0 km Option ▲▼ *Ermita Virgen del Carmen*. Depending on energy levels and daylight hours available there is an option to skip the steep climb to Villavieja and castle Corantel and go direct to Borrones as follows: ● ● ● ● ● Continue s/o past chapel over stream and up rough woodland track (faded yellow arrows) to cross  s/o [!] N-536 [0.3 km] up through quarry spill to stone workshop *Fábrica Pizarras* at **crossroads [0.4** km] *(waymarked route from Villavieja joins from left).* Proceed direct by asphalt road to **Borrones [2.1** km]. *Total 2.8 km -v- 7.5 km* uphill via Villavieja and Castillo Corantel.

▲ For the waymarked route to Villavieja turn up <right over the national road **[!] N-536 [0.3** km] continue up steeply on delightful woodland path with superb views of the countryside passing **Iglesia Villavieja [2.0** km] (right) continue s/o (left) up into **Villavieja [0.2** km].

2.5 km **Villavieja** *[F.] (CR **Cornatel** 2 night stay ✆ 619 868 122)*. Pilgrim hostel s/o up for 100m: ● *Alb. Muni.* **Manuel Fuentes** *[16÷1]* €10 ✆ 682 591 483 / 687 801 264. Original stone schoolhouse expertly converted to a pilgrim hostel with good modern facilities. Continue by *[F.]* through chestnut woods up steeply to high

point of this stage (825m). To visit the castle (recommended) turn up the path clearly signposted to side entrance and pay kiosk:

1.3 km **Castillo** *Corantel* entry gate +300m. Magnificent 9th century castle built on former Roman hill-fort. Embellished by King Alfonso VI *El Bravo* and occupied by the Templar knights in 13th century. It rivals the Templar castle in Ponferrada for its magnificence and has an unrivalled 360° viewing panorama. Diego

presides daily from 11:30–18:30 (times may fluctuate!) closed Tuesdays €2 – free with credencial. We now make our way down the asphalt road to stoneworks and **crossroads [1.6** km] *(alt. route joins from right)*. Continue down on the secondary road signposted Borrenes and at the entrance to the town (right) a shaded park with chapel and *[F.] [formerly the site of a 16th century pilgrim hospital]* continue to central **crossroads [2.1** km].

3.7 km **Borrenes** Main square with •*H* **Cornatel Médulas** *x12* €45-59 ✆ 987 420 568 (Saturno / Marisol) *www.ornatelmedulas.es* opp. *café Marisol*. South of the square on c/Arriba parish church while north on c/Abajo we pass exhibition centre *[Aula del Castaños displaying importance of the chestnut tree to both the Roman and current*

economy of the area from where flour and nut are widely exported]. Further out we pass (CR El Rincon ✆ 662 212 248 house only to let) on the way to popular restaurant Rst. Las Ventas ✆ 987 420 550 (+1.1 km on N-536)]. From Main square take the road out of town onto earth **track [1.2** km] over dry river bed and up to **crossroads [2.2** km].

3.4 km **Carucedo** *cruce opción* ▲ *[Here we have an option to alternative lodging off route*. ❶ **Carucedo**. Turn down right towards Carucedo *+400m* to •*H La Peregrina x11* €45-55 ℰ 609 062 538 *www.laperegrina.es* ❷ **Orellán** *Turn up left steeply fo*r *+2.5 km* to •*CR Louteiro* €50 ℰ 652 933 971 & •*CR O Palleiro* €40 ℰ 649 711 439].* ▲ Continue s/o along path and over Las Médulas access **road [0.4** km] back onto path and up to **road [1.6** km] *[sign for Alt. route to Orellán via mountain cycle path left]*. Continue into:

3.5 km **Las Médulas** *Turismo Aula Arqueológica* €2+ ℰ 987 422 848 *www.ieb.org.es* Open daily: 10:00–13:30 &16:00–20:00. Excellent display & information centre on the Roman gold mines adj. public car-park at the village adj. *taperia O Camiño real* with garden. (*Note: lodging in the village is limited, expensive and may require a min. 2 night stay in high season – consider staying in nearby villages*). Top end: •*H* **Medulio** *x26* €45-56 ℰ 987 422 889 *www.hotel-medulio.com* route now descends the access road (cul de sac) past ● *Alb.* **La Senda** *Priv. [10÷1]* €22 ℰ 640 244 705 Elio y Adela *www. alberguelasenda.com* – beautifully appointed hostel with shaded rear garden. •*Cabañas Rurales* **Lares** *x2* €85+ ℰ 626 108 552 *www.laresrural.com* Adj. the church •*CR* **Socorro** *x6* €20-30 ℰ 987 422 858 nearby •*CR* **Agoga** €50+ ℰ 987 422 844 *www.luralagoga.com* far end of village on track to the caves *carretera Las Cuevas* adj. *Centro de recepción de visitantes* ℰ 987 420 708 *www.turismodelbierzo.es* Open daily: 11:00–14:00 &16:00–20:00. Variety of *cafés, bars, restaurants* and souvenir shops serve this popular tourist destination.

LAS MÉDULAS: The most important gold mines in the Roman Empire. Declared a Cultural Landscape and listed by UNESCO as a World Heritage Site in 1997. The spectacular landscape of Las Médulas is the result of the mining technique called 'mountain destruction' *ruina montium*. This was

a type of hydraulic mining which involved undermining the mountain with large volumes of water that were forced into prepared galleries dug into the hillside. This water was supplied from the surrounding mountains by extensive aqueducts (up to 70 km away) that tapped the rivers and streams of La Cabrera; an area of unusually heavy rainfall. The force of the water was used to 'blast' out the side of the mountain (see photo above) and then to 'wash' the alluvial deposits for gold. This technique was described by Pliny the Elder as back as 77 C.E. when large-scale production began using up to 60,000 workers who extracted over 6,000 kg of gold annually with an estimated 1.6m kg of gold during the lifetime of the mines! The helpful staff in the display centre *Aula Arqueológica* are masters of further elaboration and information. Well worth taking the time and €2 entry fee. 1 October – 31 March: Weekdays 10:00–14:00. Saturdays: 10:00–13:30 & 15:30–18:00. Sundays: 10:00–14:00. April 1 – 30 September: Daily10:00–13:30 &16:00–20:00. ℰ 987 422 848.

A variety of delightful pathways meander through the landscape with forays into the cavernous caves. Chestnut woods predominate, a gift from the Roman occupation. Chestnuts provided a staple diet for the indigenous miners and their families. The chestnut tree *castaños* thrived on the poor soil, too steep for more conventional crops. If you don't have time or inclination for the steep climb to the Orellán viewpoint and caves we pass close to the *Mirador De Pedrices* which is worth the short (0.5 km) detour (see next stage).

REFLECTIONS:

_____
_____
_____
_____
_____
_____
_____
_____
_____
_____
_____
_____
_____
_____
_____
_____
_____
_____

Lago Sumido – Las Médulas

02 Las MÉDULAS – O BARCO
Santiago—245.6 km

┈┈┈┈	--- ---	20.5	--- ---	70%
▬▬▬▬	--- ---	8.8	--- ---	30%
▬▬▬▬	--- ---	0.0	--- ---	0%

Total km   **29.3** km (18.2 ml)

equiv. 🔺 Ascent 1,170m (+5.8 =**35.1** km)
Alto.m ▲ Option Mirador 820m (2,690 ft)
< 🅰 🅷 > Puente de Flórez **10.4** km – Sobradelo **20.4** km

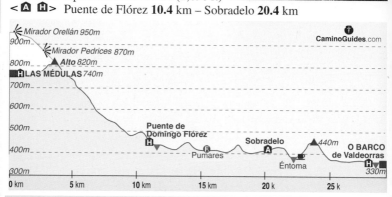

Attitude, not aptitude, determines your altitude. Zig Ziglar.

❏ **Mystical Path:** High places provide wide perspective on many different levels; our physical eyes and spiritual sight can see far-off horizons. When we are at high altitude everything below the horizon seems insignificant, even trivial. It's when we are down in the thick of the ego battleground that we fail to see the wood for the trees. Let's support each other to stay high – especially when we find ourselves lost in the darkness of lower mind.

❏ **Practical Path:** Another spectacular stage with 70% on natural paths as we descend by wide forest tracks that opens to provide a great panorama of the surrounding mountains. We have two good options for interim lodging along the sacred riverbanks *ribeira Sacra*. Notwithstanding that our first section to the río Sil is all the way downhill our *cumulative* ascent for the day is 1,175m equivalent to an extra 5.8 km of effort when compared to a level walk. Woodland provides shade from sun or shelter from rain and wind but water and sunscreen should be applied liberally.

0.0 km Las Médulas *Turismo Café H* **Medulio**. Take the road down through the village past cafés, restaurants and shops and at the end of the cul-de-sac veer right by drinking font *[F.] La Resaca* to begin our gentle climb to option:

2.3 km Opción *Mirador de Pedrices. [Detour 500m left to high viewpoint with splendid views north over Las Médulas and south over the Yeres valley].*

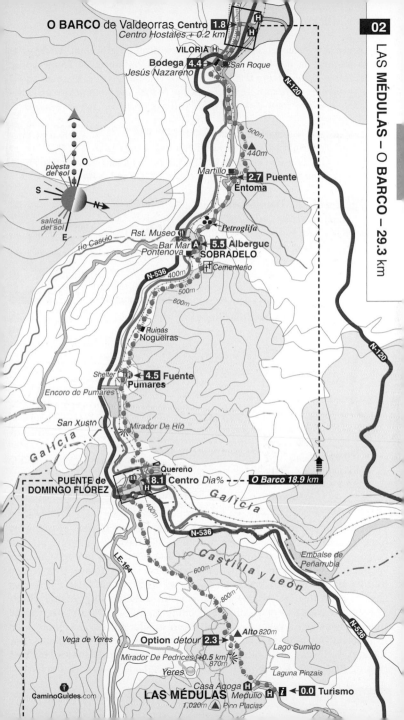

O BARCO de Valdeorras Centro **1.8** H
Centro Hostales + 0.2 km

VILORIA H
Bodega 4.4 San Roque
Jesús Nazareno

puesta
del sol
O
S
N
salida
del sol
E

río Casoyo

Martillo ▲ **2.7 Puente**
Entoma

500m
440m

Petroglifa

Rst. Museo
Bar Mar A **5.5 Alberguc**
Pontenova **SOBRADELO**
N-536 400m Cementerio
500m
600m

Ruinas
Nogueiras

Shelter **4.5 Fuente**
Pumares

Encoro de Pumares

San Xusto
Mirador De Río

Galicia

Quereno
PUENTE de **8.1 Centro** *Dia%* --- **O Barco 18.9 km**
DOMINGO FLOREZ

Galicia

400m

N-536

Castilla y León

Embalse de
Peñarrubla

LE-164
600m
800m

N-120

N-120

▲ **Alto** 820m

Vega de Yeres
Option détour 2.3
Mirador De Pedrices ⊹ **+0.5 km**
870m
Yeres

Lago Sumido

Laguna Pinzais

Casa Agoga H
LAS MÉDULAS Medulio H i **0.0 Turismo**
1,020m ▲ Pico Placias

CaminoGuides.com

Our route now takes us down a gravel track through groves of *castaños* to arrive abruptly at the **LE-164** ▲ **[7.1 km]** above Puente de Domingo de Flórez. *[If you are staying the night in town you can go directly to Hotel La Torre by turning right to roundabout on the N-536 and continue to the Hotel [0.7 km] visible by Repsol station and bridge over río Sil (see town plan).*

LE-164 ▲ the waymarked route veers left over road and down steeply on c/ Real *[F.]* right by chapel past *CR* **Casa Castañé** ℂ 686 971 766 c/ Crucero (whole house to let) and over N-536 into c/ Chao do Marco to *Dia%* *supermercado* in town centre & access to Rst. & Hotel La Torre (right).

8.1 km **Puente de Domingo Flórez**
Dia% Supermercado. •*Hs/Rst.* **La Torre II** *x17* €35-€45 ℂ 987 460 081 *www.hrlatorre.com* riverside walk to rear also •**La Torre I** *x12* €26-€45. Several restaurants ±100m off route (see town plan below). This is the last town in Castilla y León that we pass through (pop: 1,800) with all facilities incl. the hostal La Torre popular with

pilgrims. We continue over río Sil into the *province of* **Galicia** at Quereño, a quiet suburb with Endesa substation (left) and railway station (right). We pass under rail-bridge to **option [0.5 km]**. S/o right to pass through Quereño (no facilities) or left (and left again) for short-cut (saves 300m!) Both routes join by **dam wall [0.6 km]** *Embalse de Eirós* and first of several hydro electric dams that we pass as we journey down the río Sil. We now climb steeply above railway onto delightful path through forest passing **viewpoint [0.6 km]** over the Sil valley to descend sharply under railway and climb again to a second **viewpoint [1.2 km]** with bench seat (see photo 'Reflections'). The forest path follows the contour into the quaint village of **Pumares [1.3 km]** passing *Bodega A Dega* to main square at far end and water font **[0.3 km]**.

4.5 km **Pumares Plaza Estella** with covered shelter (left) opposite *[F.]*. We now have a wonderful 5 kilometre of path and track parallel to the river and railway below us (left) passing the ruins of **Nogueiras [2.1** km] an abandoned village with level-crossing and ruin turned into open shelter *Bienvenido a Tu Casa* and statue of the Virgin Mary. We pass **picnic area** and climb through dense forest of *castaños* past cemetery into the top *alto* of Sobradelo **[3.4** km].

5.5 km **Sobradelo** *alto café Pontenova* (left) opp. *Bar Mar* with terrace and ● *Alb.* **Mar** *Priv.[35÷8]* €15 ℰ 988 335 106 where Manuel welcomes pilgrims to refurbished hostal with all facilities incl. washing/ drying. *[Note: camino continues up past hostel entrance. If you want to visit the river and 7 arch medieval bridge XVIc. (Roman foundations)*  *descend down steeply to* **Sobradelo** *bajo (pop: 650) with Rst. Museo on far side of river].* The waymarked route continues *up* the main road past the *Casa Consistorial* with viewpoint over the bridge and then maintains the high contour alongside the busy secondary road with narrow margins [!] passing **Petroglifa [1.5** km] (left) 50m with poor access. We take the next access road (right) down steeply into **Éntoma [1.2** km].

2.7 km **Éntoma** *Puente* medieval bridge (Roman origin) over río Galir and just beyond we find *[F.]* (left) and *Bar Martillo* with terrace fronting the road. Small town (pop: 400) with several wineries *bodegas* mostly of Godello grape variety. We leave by forest path that bids us *Bo Camiño* clearly proud of its Galician heritage and D.O wines and ascend to our high point of this stage at a mere 440m to start our descent towards **O Barco** crossing main road [!] and down *under* **rail bridge [3.6** km] onto track by river, our low point at 320m. We now wind our way back up over rail and turn down left into rúa Virxe da Barxa to **Bodega [0.8** km].

4.4 km **Bodega** *Cooperativa Jesús Nazareno* (tours/visitors) opp. *Bar S. Roque.* *[Note: we still have 2.0 km to cover to lodging in the town centre (and 5.1 km if you staying at the albergue the far side of town). Waymarking is generally good but stay focussed through this delightful but busy town].* We pass several bars on our way to the **N-536 [0.6** km] [!]

◆ Note also: bridge over the río Sil (left) to suburb of **Viloira** with several hostals and restaurants. Most pilgrims stay this side of the river but if lodging is scarce or you want to explore off-route, this is the place to cross: **VILOIRA** ± ½ km [± €30]: •*P******O'Isla** ℰ 647 278 318 / 678 480 009 Av. Elena Quiroga, 6 (adj. bridge). •*P&Rst.* **Viloira** ℰ 988 322 152 Plaza Oerto Pedrayo 13. •*P* **A Barca** ℰ 699 366 085 c/ Elena Quiroga 27.

◆ Cross N-536 into historic part of **O Barco** *Casco Vello* along ruas

San Roque and Real past houses emblazoned with family crests onto the lovely riverside walk *paseo fluvial* **Parque do Malecón [0.4 km]** with the first of many cafes and bars that line this pedestrian walkway with *Xanadu* (credencial) and *Pasarela* opp. pedestrian bridge *pasarela* over the river which leads to a delightful alternative 'green' path to A Rua (see next stage). We continue to: **[0.8 km]**

1.8 km **O Barco** *de Valdeorra Opción.* Information board *Camiño de Inverno* (*Galego* spelling). The route has at last (thankfully) been waymarked along the riverside. This is the point we need to veer right into the town centre for lodging and / or ***albergue at Xagoaza*** ✪ *(+3.1 km) see next page.*

The old town *casco vello* is centred around the Royal Way *Rua Real* a continuation of the *Rua San Roque* which provides another link to the medieval pilgrim way. Today the town is centred around its modern shops and squares but the real heart of town is the riverside promenade *Parque do Malecón* where numerous bars and cafés spill out onto the leafy *paseo* and, in summer, musicians and street artists add to the lively café culture. At **option point** (end of Parque do Malecón *Camiño de Inverno* information board) either continue s/o along the riverside for stage 3 or turn into town for lodging and alternative road route with access to the albergue in Xagoaza.

Behind bar *Pasarela* on the paseo is the newly built ❶ *H*° **Malecon** *x18* €45+ © 988 684 932 on Rúa Pescadores, 3. Continue over roundabout into **rua Orense** *bar Galileo* (right) to crossroads **Av. Conde de Fenosa** ❖ (150m) turn right for ❷ *Hs* **La Gran Tortuga** *x6* (The Big Tortoise) (50m left) at N°37 €25-35 © 988 347 044 [m] 608 573 480 *www.lagrantortuga.com* ❖ Continue s/o into **Rua Castelao** and turn left into **Av. Eulogio Fernández** (150m) to

❸ *H°* **Mayo** *x15* €25-35 ⓒ 988 322 098 *www.hostalmayo.es* @ N°70. S/o to next crossroads (Rúa Penas Forcadas) to popular ❹ *P°°***do Lar** *x9* €35-45 ⓒ 988 320 980 above *Rst. Cocina do Lar*. Nearby c/Xirmil,3 ❺ *P°°***Aurum** *x4* ±€40 ⓒ 988 108 416 *www.aurumpension.com* *(+1.5 km)* in **Vila do Castro** ❻ *H°°°***Pazo Do Castro** €60 ⓒ 988 347 423 also in the area on N-120 modern ❼ *H°°°* **O Camiño** *x40* €50-80 ⓒ 988 322 686 *www.hotelocamino.es* *(+1.4 km)* off route North of Castro ● *Alb. Peregrinos* **Xagoaza** (see next stage).

O Barco de Valdeorras *The Boat [across] the Valley of Gold*. 2 millennia ago the Romans came to extract gold all along this valley (not just at Las Médulas). Today the area is renowned for its slate quarries where roofing slate is exported from here throughout Europe and is one of the major employment activities of the town (overall pop; 12,000). Wine production makes the other great contribution to the area. All along the riverside *Ribeira Sacra* we see vineyards stretching up the steep slopes. Valdeorras is a respected *denominación de origen* D.O. One of its most popular wines is fruity white from the Godello grape variety.

REFLECTIONS:

_____
_____
_____
_____
_____
_____
_____
_____
_____

Río Sil – Ribeira Sacra

03 O BARCO – A RUA (Alta)
Santiago—216.3 km

ııııııııııı	--- ---	5.2	--- ---	*40%*
	--- ---	8.0	--- ---	*60%*
	--- ---	0.0	--- ---	
Total km		**13.2** km (8.2 ml)		

equiv.
▲ Ascent 570m (+2.9=**16.1** km)
Alto.m ▲ Cruceiro 350m (1,150 ft)
<Ⓐ Ⓗ> Vilamartín **7.5** km.

400m — *H*.Berna
O BARCO   Vilamartín   350m ┼ A RUA   Ⓗ
■300m   Ⓐ   Ⓐ
0 km   5 km   10 km   13.2 km

Everything; mountains, rivers, trees should be our teacher. *Morihei Ueshiba*

❏ **Mystical Path:** Life is a camino and, like a river, never static but in constant flow. We start with a trickle that builds momentum as we rush down the mountainside of our life navigating narrow gorges and opening to smoother waters beyond. We finally arrive back to the Source which is nothing less than a merging with the Ocean of Oneness. This is the essence of Who we are, our Numinous Self that has been hidden behind clouds of forgetfulness. It was those clouds that fell to the earth as separate raindrops initiating the whole process of individual incarnation. The cycle ends when the clouds no longer form in our mind.

❏ **Practical Path:** The *main route* Ⓐ out of O Barco has recently been waymarked via a delightful river path. This makes for a short and easy stage to prepare for the more demanding days that follow. The route is level along the narrow valley that we share with the N-12 and railway. There is an option to use the peaceful *camino natura* Ⓑ on the far side of the river which avoids the busy main road and makes a delightful alternative. It rejoins the main route in Vilamartín which makes a good midway rest area on the river (photo above). The third option is to take the original route to **Veigamuiños** Ⓒ and detour to the albergue in *Xagoaza* Ⓧ. Bring a snack for each option as the only café en route is Vilamartín 250m *off* route.

Ⓒ **Original road route** ● ● ● ● *via* **Veigamuiños** rejoins new river route at roundabout with **Detour to Xagoaza** ● ● ● ● ●*Alb. Peregrinos* **Xagoaza** *Muni [36÷2]* €6 Ⓒ Gloria 639 921 679 converted school (see photo>) with steep climb (500m) overlooking the peace-filled río Mariñán valley 3.1 km North of O Barco. On the *far* side of

Petín
Puente A Cigarrosa
OU-536
N-120 Berna [+ 1.4 km]
Fabio Sanchez
Encoro de San Martiño
Polideportivo
A
S.María
Alta
Solaina
2.5 Fontei Igrexa
H Pillabán
A RUA de VALDEORRAS
Taxi P
Concello
Baja
Esplada H
OU-536
300m
Alto 350m
Vilela
C Pacio Do Sil + 300m
S.Roque 3.2 P.S.Roque
Capela S.Roque

Santiago
Valencia do Sil
Presa de Santiago
N-120
1,000 m
500 m
P Marbella + 500m
Vilamartín
A 1.0 Albergue piscina
Vilamartín
Penouta
Covas
H A Lastra + 200m
3.4 4.2 Pasarela unión
Valdegodos
H Paladium + 750m
H Calzada + 700m
Arcos
Córgomo
400 m
Fervenza
S.Xoan
Arnado
Pazo arco 3.9 ruinas
500 m
S.Mariña
do Monte
Vales
Industrial
500 m
Gadis
300m
2.3 1.4 Rotonda unión
A Raña
A Proba
Sunset
W
S
Igrexa y Mosterio
S.Miguel de Xagoaza
Bodegas
Godeval
As Hortas
O Ferradal
Sunrise
E
B
río Mariñao
A
Veigamuiños
N-536
N-120
río Mariñao
1.7 Puente
Termiña
★ 0.0
Hs
O Lar
Xagoaza
C
Albergue 1.4 A
O BARCO
de VALDEORRAS
Hs Gran Tortuga
Estación
H Camiño
Pacios
H Viloira

CaminoGuides.com

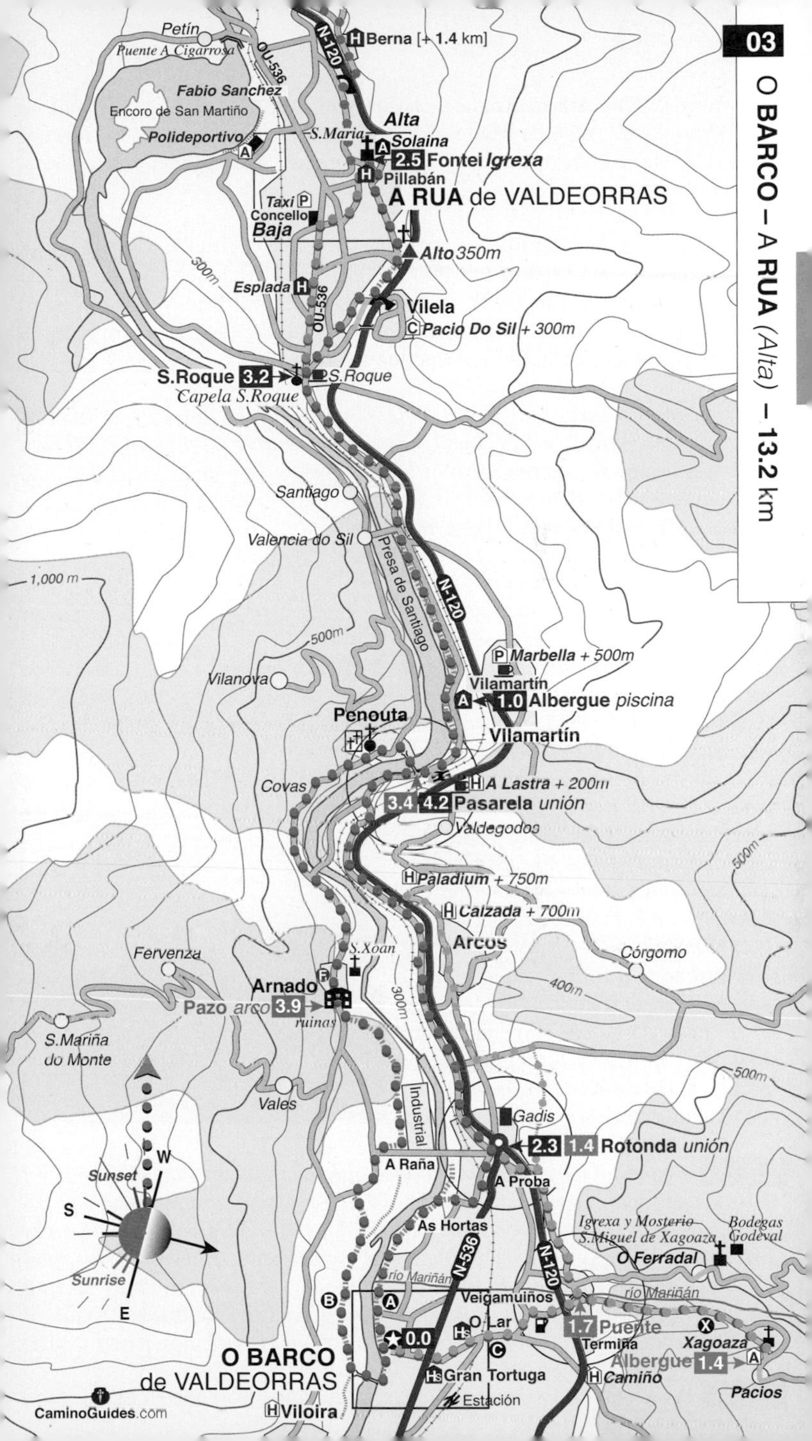

the valley is **Monasterio Xagoaza** *XVIIIc.* adj. the Romanesque **Iglesia de San Miguel** *XIIc.* with its Maltese cross, symbol of the Order of St. John of Jerusalem carved above the door and its Knights Hospitallers connections. For this alt. route proceed as follows:

`0.0 km` **Option** ❸ **Camiño Inverno info. board** ✪ head into town on c/ Ourense, over main road & left into Av. Eulogio Fernández passing Hostal Mayo (right) and O Lar (left) continue s/o under rail into Veigamuiños & left at roundabout (opp. Galp) and right into Camiño Xagoazas (opp. mod. church) s/o under N-120 to Termiña **puente**. ◆

`1.7 km` **Puente** *Termiña*. *[Detour (signposted) to Alb.* **Xagoaza** ● ● ● ● *Keep s/o up steeply to* **albergue** *[1.4 km] opp. church. no facilities].* Return and cross bridge ◆ into rua Termiña and follow country lanes towards *Gadis* sign and cross N-120 on flyover *[old route into Arcos s/o at this point]* into **A Pobra** down to roundabout where other route joins from left.

`1.4 km` **A Pobra Rotonda** *unión.*

`0.0 km` **Option** ❸ *camino natura* ● ● ● ● *[7.3 km -v- 6.5 km]* avoids the newly waymarked route that runs imm. parallel to the busy N-120 to Vilamartín. **At Camiño Inverno info. board** ✪ turn back down Parque do Malecón to *bar Pasarela* and cross footbridge *pasarela* over río Sil and continue through park passing first of several dark red local walking signs *camino natural km 30 [0.5 km]* and turn **up left [0.1 km]** (*not* s/o right by river) and turn right along **road [1.3 km]** and turn down towards bridge (*not* s/o along the circuit *Ruta da Pincheira de Portomao* via Fervenza). Take the track imm. to the left of the road bridge and follow along side of industrial estate (far side of a drainage ditch) into woodland and back onto **road [1.6 km]** and turn under arch through **Pazo de Arnado [0.4 km]** an abandoned stately home (photo>).

`3.9 km` **Arnado** *Arco de Pazo Arnado.* Continue past capela (right) and *[F.]* (left) ancient hamlet with no facilities. S/o along quiet country lane (Igrexa San Xoan right) up into woodlands around **Covas** *[bodegas built into caves in the side of the cliffs]* up to **Penouta** chapel and cemetery. *[The road continues into Valencia do Sil by dam]* but we join the main route by turning down steeply in Penouta to cross over river. Cross the footbridge *pasarela* (see photo under reflections) and pick up official waymark *mojón* on far side.

`3.4 km` **Pasarela** *unión Vilamartín* main route joins from the right.

`0.0 km` **Option ❹ Camiño Inverno info. board ❺** continue along riverside over culvert (río Mariñán) through woodland past water treatment plant *Edar* and take next right (not s/o) into old suburb of As Hortas and left at roundabout on Av. de Galicia over rail and up to second roundabout at junction of N-536 and N-120 and *Gadis hipermarket* where alternative route from Xagoaza joins from right.

`2.3 km` **Rotonda** *A Proba unión* we now take a secondary road alongside the N-120 past *[Detour right [2.5 km] Arcos •H**Calzada x12 €45-60 ℂ 888 040 012 www.hotelcalzada.es c/ Calzada (+700m). Also •H***Palladium x28 €49-66 ℂ 988 33 68 01 paladiumvaldeorras.es]*. Keep s/o alongside N-120 past slate factory *Pizarras Gallegas* to turn left over railway **[1.0** km] down to river at **footbridge [0.7** km].

`4.2 km` **Pasarela** *Vilamartín**✱** [Detour right (200m) N-120 •H A Lastra x12 €18-€36 ℂ 988 300 232 m: Clemente 626 391 906 www.hotelalastra. com directly on N-120. **Directions** for A Lastra turn up sharp right alongside railway and cross over [!] at Villamartín de Valdeorras estación]. ✱ continue from pasarela by río Sil and over a tributary río Leira **Puente de Santiago** by Mirador Río and riverside walkway pista al río shaded by trees and lined with picnic benches past sports ground to municipal swimming pool with adjoining albergue.

`1.0 km` **Albergue** *Vilamartín*. Take the path to rear of the swimming-pool ● *Alb.* **Vilamartín** *Muni [44÷2] €8 ℂ Salvador 680 602 423/ 679 846 879. [Detour: +500m cross under railway and over N-120 to village centre with café, shop & •Hs/Rst.* **Marbella** *℗ 988 300 025 on r/ Miguel de Cervantes].* Keep s/o country road between rail

(right) and river (left) to dam *presa* **Presa de Santiago [1.6** km] s/o up parallel to N-120 with panoramic views down the Sil valley to the outskirts of **A Rua de Valdeorras** at **San Roque [1.6** km].

`3.2 km` **San Roque** *Rua de Valdeorras*. Capela San Roque opp. *bar S. Roque*. A sign ❑ (see photo) indicates option *Rua Alta* up right to follow waymarks to the old *viejo* town *(note private albergue Solaina is now closed)* or s/o for the lower modern town *Rua Baja* with municipal albergue in the sports hall *polideportivo* by lake (1.2 km *off* route).

❑ For the route into the modern 'lower' end of town keep s/o along the main

road OU-356 past ❶ *H*****Espada** *x47* basic rooms from €35 ℂ 988 310 075 (r/Campo Grande 44) into r/ do Progreso to town centre and **Concello A Rúa** ℂ 988 310 116 (check-in for albergue) Praza José Antonio Míguez Freire. Wide range of shops, cafés, restaurants and **lodging:** To rear of Concello ❷ *P& Rst.* **O Taxi** ℂ 988 310 411 r/ Circunvalación, 70. ❸ *Hs* **Niza** *x10* €35 ℂ 988 310 807 r/ Doutor Vila, 30 with bar *A Eskina* on the corner. ❹ *P******Fabio Sanchez** *x22* €25 ℂ 636 897 217 *www.pensionfabio.es* r/ do Progreso, 202. ❺ *Alb.* **Polideportivo** *Muni. [20÷2]* €8 ℂ 988 310 116 sports hall (**+1.2** km from Concello) by reservoir *Encoro de S.Martiño* (photo top). On the far side of the lake is the medieval bridge *Puente A Cigarrosa* linking A Rua to Petín of Roman origin and part of the Via XVIII from Braga to Astorga it was rebuilt in the sixteenth century (**+1.5** km from Concello). If you are staying in the lower town area it is easier to return to the waymarked route in upper town via r/ Telesforo Ojea (*bar Retorno*) directly opp. the Concello. This leads to the emblematic Igrexa N.S. Fátima in Fontei.

❏ For the main waymarked route to the old town *Alta* turn up right through **Praza César Conti [0.4** km] *bar Novo* **Igrexa de San Estevo** with statue of Santiago Peregrino. *[The adj. house has a stone portico and pays tribute to a Roman officer who lived here]*. Turn right into r/ O Bouzo past Casa El Bouzo (red balcony) to T-junction *[right turn for alt. route to Pacio Sil]* turn left up to **underpass [0.7** km] under N-120 and road route to *[*❻ *CR* **Pacio Do Sil** *x10* €60+ ℂ 988 311 346 *www.paciodosil.es* r/ Xestal 33 in **Vilela** (*+300m)]*. Take the path alongside the N-120 *above* and over crossroads up to high point by roadside cross *cruceiro*. We now follow waymarks *down* into 'old' A Rua (alta) where several narrow lanes meet at **junction [1.2** km] Here signs point right to albergue (+50m) ❼ *Alb.* **Casa da Solaina** *Priv.* ℂ m: 616 124 521 Plaza do Santo. Asún, a naturopath with a love of the camino provides information on the *Inverno* route but no longer provides beds. Plans to refurbish the derelict chapel in the adj. square are also on hold *[Roman Milestone **Miliario Romano** from the first century, part of the Via XVIII Bracara Augusta (Braga) to Asturica Augusta (Astorga) adjoins the chapel]*. Continue left to **church [0.2** km] on Praza Enriqueta Casanova.

2.5 km A Rua *Alta Igrexa N.S. Fátima Fontei* ❽ *HsRst.* **O Pillabán** *x5* €20-40 ℂ 988 311 416 (see photo with church in background>) **Iglesia de A Nosa Señora de Fátima –** *Fontei* the church has a handsome stone façade with prominent twin towers. *[It appears Gaudí was a regular summer visitor to A Rua and attended services*

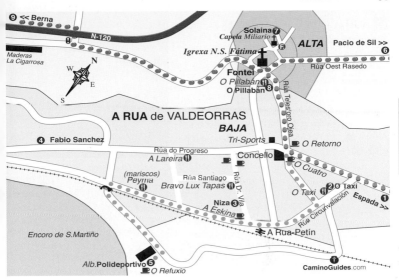

in the church. He is reputed to have made recommendations to its redesign and the stained glass]. The next stage to Quiroga is a long day and if you want to get a head start you could overnight at hotel **❾ H Berna** *x42* €20+ *©* 988 310 124 on way out of town and directly on the camino a further 1.4 km from the church at ***Fontei*** (see next stage for details).

REFLECTIONS:

_____

_____

_____

_____

_____

_____

Vilamartín – Pasarela (alternativo via camino naturales).

04 A RUA (Alta) – QUIROGA
Santiago—203.1 km

/////////	--- ---	9.2	--- ---	*32%*
══════	--- ---	19.2	--- ---	*68 %*
▬▬▬	--- ---	<u>0.0</u>	--- ---	
Total km		**28.4 km** (17.6 ml)		

equiv. ▲ Ascent 1,480 m (+7.4=**35.8** km)

Alto.m ▲ O Albaredos 505 m (1,656 ft)

< 🅰 🇭 > Soldón **21.1** km.

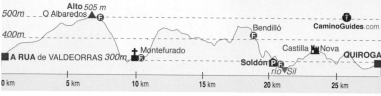

A picture is a poem without words. Horace

An old adage suggests that a picture is worth a thousand words. We can portray things with shape and colour that we couldn't so easily impart any other way. Today our long and isolated path through the woods is strewn with images that keep us company and evoke a range of emotions and reflections. The flag of  Galicia is a blue St Andrew's Cross over a white field. Andrew is a popular Galician saint and also patron saint of Scotland whose flag also bears his cross. Scottish DNA is rooted to the Galician Celts. A coincidence stranger than fiction.

❏ **Practical Path:** A long (35.8 km allowing for cumulative ascent) and remote stage. Facilities en route are limited to a few water fonts with no cafés except a summer cantina in Soldón. Fill up water flasks & energy snacks before leaving town. We start in the upper part of A Rua *alta* at the church in Fontei alt. 290m (adj. Solaina) and proceed up and *under* [!] the N-120 to our high point at 505m in O Albaredos. We now enter the province of Lugo and while 68% is on asphalt there is little or no traffic on the secondary roads and the way is relieved by colourful artwork. Our way meanders through peaceful pine forest with extensive views down over the Sil valley.

0.0 km A Rua *Alta* Fontei *Igrexa N.S. Fátima Rst.Pension* O Pillabán. Continue up past the church *[waymark dedicated to Ramón García Rodríguez president of the local camino association]*. Turn right> under **tunnel [0.7 km]** and take track sharp <left for another **[0.7 km]** to:

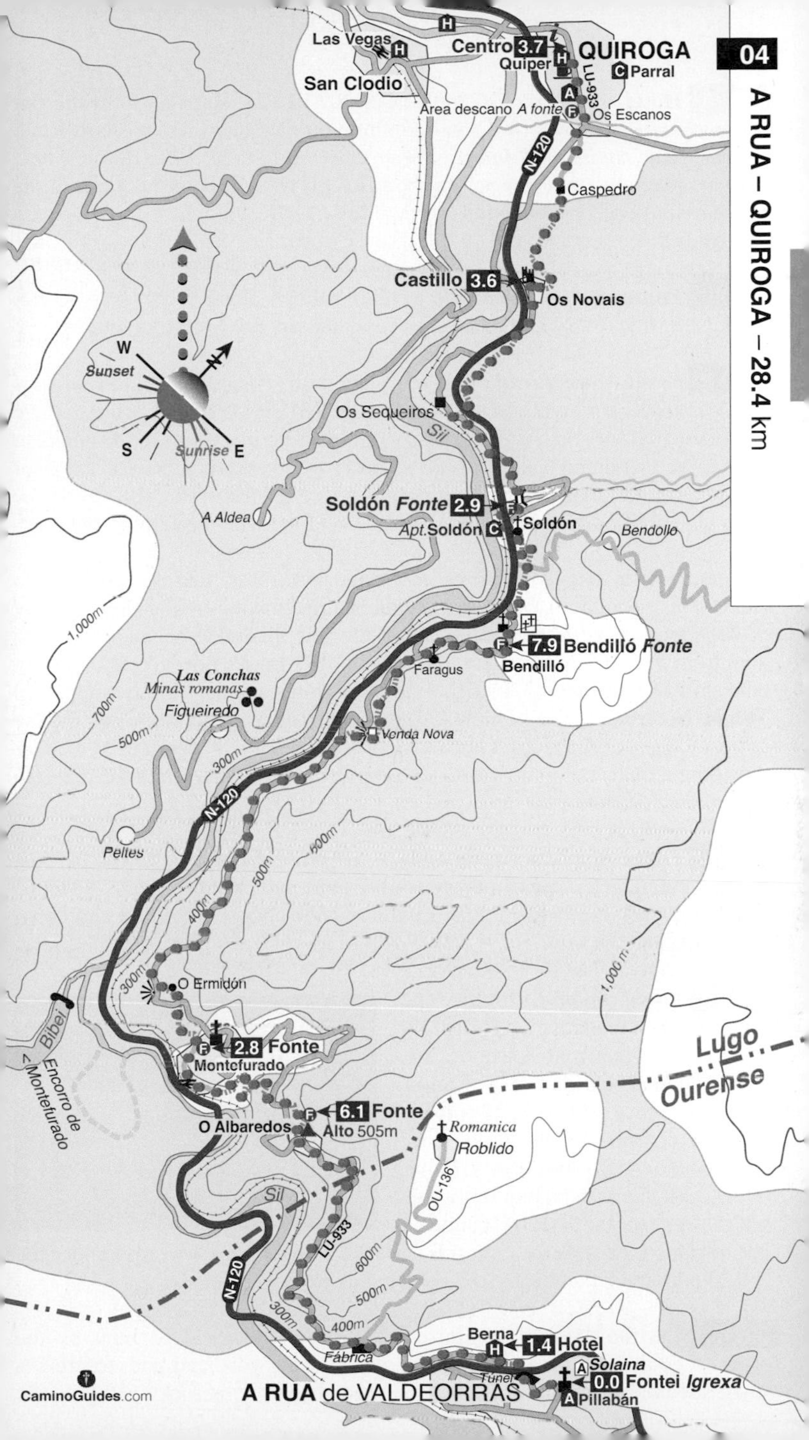

H Las Vegas **H**
Centro **3.7** **QUIROGA**
San Clodio Quiper **C** Parral
A
Area descano *A fonte* **F** LU-933
Os Escanos

Caspedro

Castillo **3.6** **H**
Os Novais

Os Sequeiros

Soldón *Fonte* **2.9** **H**
Apt.Soldón **C** **†** **Soldón**
Bendollo

F **7.9** Bendilló *Fonte*
Faragus **Bendilló** **†**

W
Sunset
S
Sunrise E

A Aldea

Las Conchas
Minas romanas
Figueiredo

Venda Nova

N-120

Pelles

O Ermidón

F **2.8** Fonte
Montefurado

F **6.1** Fonte
O Albaredos Alto 505m

Romanica
† *Roblido*

OU-136

Lugo
Ourense

Sil

LU-933

N-120

Berna
H **1.4** Hotel
Fábrica **A** *Solaina*
A **0.0** Fontei *Igrexa*
A RUA de VALDEORRAS **A** Pillabán
Túnel

1.4 km **Hotel** •*H* **Berna** *x42* €20+ © 988 310 124. Keep s/o past the fire station *Bomberos* down (left) and continue up past factories on sharp bend. *[Local road (right) to Robildo a mountain village with XIIc. Romanesque church].* Keep s/o up (view of dam on río Sil) to high point at 505m in the remote village of **O Albaredos** (no facilities). On leaving the village we pass *[F.]* (right):

6.1 km **Fonte** *O Albaredos*. We continue down along forest path to rail track alongside río Sil and past rail station and up into Montefurado:

2.8 km **Fonte** *Montefurado* village square with *[F.]* and imposing church of *San Miguel XVIIIc.* with its red stone walls and elevated belfry. The village is named after a tunnel, a 2nd century engineering marvel of the Romans to 'pierce the mountain' *monte furado* in order to divert the course of the river to extract gold (similar to the process at Las Médulas). The village is now semi-abandoned awaiting, perhaps, a revival along with the camino Invierno.

We continue up steeply on forest track and just before taking the road into *Hermidón* we can look back and see the río Sil flowing by the Roman *túnel de Montefurado* with the confluence of the ríos Sil and Bibei and the hydro dam from *Encorro de Montefurado* just out of sight. We now take the country lane into **O Ermidón [1.1** km]. Continue along contour line to signboard **Venda Novas [3.9** km] which displays the Roman gold workings on the opposite bank of the river. The stacks of loose boulders were left over after the alluvial mud containing gold deposits was washed out. Continue down to the isolated chapel of Farrapas and up into **Bendilló** *[F.]* **[2.9** km].

7.9 km **Fonte** *Bendilló* (water only – no other facilities). Continue past parish church (left) and cemetery (right) onto path which zigzags down to cross over the N-120 **[!]** and past small roadside chapel in **Soldón** and down to river basin.

2.9 km **Fonte** *Soldón*. Idyllic spot (except for the viaduct!) by río Sil and small waterfront harbour area with picnic tables and *[F.]*. Cantina (summer only). •*Apt.***O Muiño** *x5* €50 per apartment (see photo opp.) © Luis: 679 455 126 Maria: 679 467 032. Cross the river and up onto short 500m stretch of the N-120 **[!]** and veer

left towards (not into) the riverside village of **Sequeiros**. We cross under the N-120 onto track that becomes asphalted as we enter **Novais:**

3.6 km **Castillo** *Novais* prominent 12th century tower (left) built by the order of Saint John of Jerusalem. We descend by woodland path to cross a small stream over medieval bridge and ascend sharply by rocky path into the picturesque village of **Caspedro [1.4** km]. *[in the Middle Ages the camino took a track (right) towards San Xulián de Arriba where there was a pilgrim hospital].* We leave via the hermitage of Santo Antonio and O Pazo Vello to crossroads and cross over **bridge [1.1** km] with rest area (left) *[F.] área de descanso A Fonte* and s/o up *Calle Real* past (right) *Bar/Rst. Matrioshka pilgrim stamp from Irina, Alexandr & Olga* and left **albergue [0.6** km] ● *Alb.* **Quiroga** *Muni [150÷22]* €10 ✆ 982 428 166 <u>www.tourgalia.com</u> (open to youth groups which can be noisy!) and up to Hostal Quiper in the centre of **Quiroga [0.6** km].

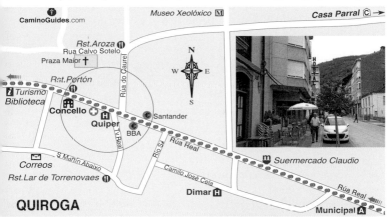

3.7 km Centro *Quiroga*. •*Hs* **Quiper** *x7* €17-30 ✆ 982 428 451 Esther Soto Pérez 676 110 961 above popular *Café Quiper*. **Other Lodging:** •*Hs.Rst.* **Dimar** *(Matías) x6* €15-25 ✆ 669 297 760 r/ Camilo José Cela, 14. •**Casa do Parral** *x2* €25 Pacios de Mondelo ✆ 669 399 362. (Hotel Marcos c/ Secide closed) opp. popular *Rst. Aroza* ✆ 982 428 447 r/ Calvo Sotelo, 13. *[See also next stage for •H.* **Las Vegas** *[+2.1 km via LU-651] and •Hs* **Remansiño** *[+1.1 km via LU-933].*

05 QUIROGA – MONFORTE de LEMOS
Santiago—174.7 km

'''''''''''''''''''	--- ---	19.1	--- ---	*52%*
════════	--- ---	17.8	--- ---	*48 %*
▬▬▬▬	--- ---	<u>0.0</u>	--- ---	
Total km		**36.9 km (22.9 ml)**		

▲ *equiv.* Ascent 1,890 m (+9.4= **46.3** km!)

Alto.*m* ▲ Alto 605 m (1,985 ft)

< Ⓐ Ⓗ > San Clodio **2.1** km – A Ponte **16.6** – A Pobra do Brollón **24.1** km

Immerse yourself in the outdoor experience. It will cleanse your soul.

Fred Bear

❏ **Mystical Path:** Nikola Tesla suggested that ideas, like the mountains we climb, at first cause discomfort and we become anxious to get down, distrustful of our own powers to cope successfully. But soon the remoteness from the turmoil of life and the inspiring influence of the altitude calm us and our steps get firm and sure and we begin to look for even dizzier heights. Will we allow ourselves to merge with the remoteness of the path and allow the energy of the Landscape Temple to draw us forward. Tiredness takes hold in the mind... as does vim and vigour.

❏ **Practical Path:** This is the longest and most arduous stage on the Winter Way with an ascent of 1,890m (equivalent of 46.9 km!) it involves 3 steep climbs out of the Sil, Lor and Saá river valleys (see contour guide above). There are few facilities on route so stock up with water and energy snacks before leaving Quiroga and consider breaking the journey at Pobra do Brollón or several *off* route options. Shortly after leaving Quiroga we leave the Sil river valley to climb to our high point at 605m in the mountains surrounding the remote Capela dos Remedios. Over half the route is on natural paths.

0.0 km Centro *Quiroga Hs* **Quiper** s/o up main street past *Casa do Concello & Turismo* & library and *supermercado Plenus* down under the N-120 to bridge over the río Sil and **option [0.9 km]** ▲

*[For **alternative** (600m shorter) route by busy and narrow LU-933 keep s/o at bridge past •H **Remansiño** x10 €35 © 982 435 168 on main road but with rear boundary on river. Continue to **next** road bridge where the new waymarked route joins from the left 1.1 km (total 2.0 km -v- 2.6 km via main route)].*

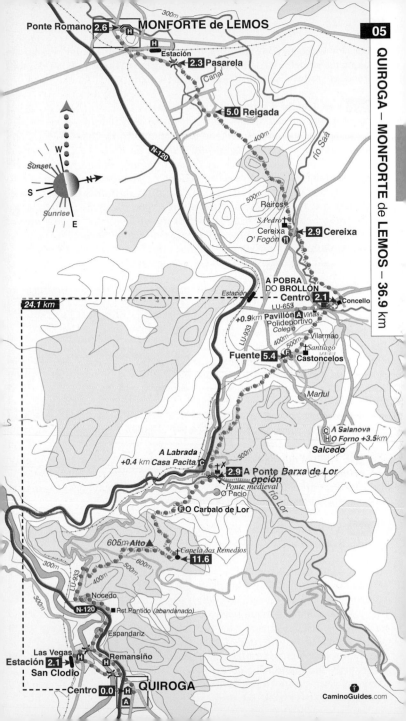

Ponte Romano **2.6** MONFORTE de LEMOS

Estación

2.3 Pasarela

Canal

5.0 Reigada

400m

río Saá

500m

Rairos

S. Pedro

Cereixa **2.9** Cereixa
O' Fogón

A POBRA
DO BROLLÓN
Centro **2.1**

Estación

Concello

LU-653

+0.9km Pavillón A Viñas
Polideportivo
Colegio

400m 500m Vilarmao

Santiago
Fuente **5.4** Castoncelos

Martul

A Salanova
O Forno +3.5km
Salcedo

A Labrada
+0.4 km Casa Pacita C

2.9 A Ponte Barxa de Lor
opción
Ponte medieval
O Pacio

río Lor

O Carbalo de Lor

605m Alto
Capela dos Remedios
600m **11.6**

500m

400m

Nocedo

N-120 Rst. Pontido (abandanado)

Espandariz

Las Vegas
Estación **2.1** Remansiño
San Clodio

Centro **0.0** QUIROGA

24.1 km

N-120

LU-933

300m

CaminoGuides.com

▲ For new waymarked route turn left at the bridge option point *over* the río Sil along the straight rua do Sil and turn left at **plaza Mayor [1.0** km] to *cafés & Hotel* adj. railway station at **San Clodio [0.2** km].

2.1 km San Clodio *Estación* •*H.*Las Vegas *x14* €22 © 982 428 283 r/ Ferrocarril opp. rail station. Several *cafés* adjoin. Continue alongside railway past cafés *A Cabina* and *Río Sil* and turn right down by *supermercado San Clodio (last chance to buy food before A Pobra do Brollón 22.0 km)* into r/ da Liberdade past *café Dickens (last chance saloon)* and back over the **río Sil [0.5** km] to rejoin the alternative road route. We now continue parallel to the river and N-120 through Espandariz and through **tunnel [1.5** km] under the N-120 to abandoned Rst./disco **Pontido**. *[Note: this is the point we leave the Sil valley at 300m and head up steeply to our high point of this stage at 605m. The climb is rewarded with fine views along the remote and peaceful woodland paths but there are NO facilities on this stretch until we reach a water font and covered rest area in O Carbalo de Lor 10.5 km away].*

Continue past turning for **Nocedo [0.6** km] (loud dogs) and watch out for waymark for sharp right turn onto the start of the **forest track [2.4** km] through pine woods. Cross road **[2.1** km] to reach our high point for this stage *Alto 605m* **[1.0** km] we now start our descent into the Lor river valley taking a sharp right hand bend over **río Maior [1.5** km] to woodland  cross-tracks at **Capela dos Remedios** *XVIIc.* **[2.0** km]. (see photo above)

11.6 km Capela *dos Remedios* We continue our descent into the hamlet of **O Carbalo de Lor** with covered rest area and *[F]*. Keep s/o down towards the Lor river with fine views and pass a small hamlet (loud dogs) to arrive at the magnificent medieval bridge **A Ponte** over the río Lor.

2.9 km A Ponte Barxa *río Lor Opción.* Keep s/o or left for detour:

[Detour +350m to welcoming café and •*P.* Pacita *x5* €25-35 © 982 430 008 in Labrada de Lor. Turn immediately left over the bridge along tranquil riverside track to the road overpass with the petite Pacita tucked in underneath. The flyover is so high the traffic makes  surprisingly little noise. If you are overnighting there is a delightful walk along the river, *up*stream of the bridge, by ruined building to a fisherman's track along the river bank (see map).

Continue up past *Igrexa de Santa Mariña de Barxa de Lor* and cemetery and watch carefully for the **waymark s/o up [0.4** km] to leave the road at this point on track and keep s/o again at country road **junction [0.3** km] (pylon left) onto a track that winds its way through woodland to T-Junction **[4.3** km] onto asphalt road. *[Signpost right direct to accommodation at Salcedo 3.6 km (details next paragraph)]* keep s/o into **Castroncelos [0.4** km] with covered rest area and *[F]*.

5.4 km **Castroncelos** *Fuente opción [Detour: +3.6 km to Salcedo off route lodging: Take farm track opp. fuente into Martul 1.2 km & Salcedo 2.3 km (total 3.6 km) or continue into A Pobra do Brollón & arrange free pickup from there. •H**O Forno x12 €35-45 © 982 430 501 [m] 619 813 834 José Luis www.turismoruralensalcedo.net with restaurant and swimming pool. Also part of •CR**A Salanova x10 €30-35 on adj. c/ Carreira. Cantina de Julia serves meals. You can arrange for your hosts to drop you back on the camino in the morning... or walk].* Keep s/o through the tiny hamlet of **Castroncelos** past turning for *[Igrexa Santiago 200m off route right]* through Vilarmao and back onto farm track onto road in the suburbs of A Pobra. Turn left on road and imm. right (50m) down over a small stream and picturesque picnic area. Good place to refresh tired feet? Continue over river Saá by park *Área recreativa de Sanugueiros* and up to popular *café* (first for 22 kilometres!) on Av. Galicia. The albergue is on the outskirts of the village (left) but we are close to the Concello for information and check-in. Continue right along the main street right past ✚ *farmacia* (right) and *Rst. Avenida* to crossroads. ✚

2.1 km **A Pobra do Brollón** *Concello* council and locals are welcoming and clearly want to support pilgrims and the town makes an ideal stage ending. The Mayor is very supportive and lodging is available in the sports hall.

●*Alb. Muni [12 : 1]* **Polideportivo** €-donativo © 638 276 855 / Xose Gago 666 435 832. *Directions: Head back down Av. Galicia past recreation park and supermarket to roundabout (300m) and keep s/o past pension Viñas (currently closed) to large college left and sports pavilion to rear (600m) total 0.9 km].*

✚ At crossroads take the road left (opp. Concello) onto tree-lined farm track alongside the río Saá to **detour [2.0** km]. *[Detour 200m right signposted to archaeological excavations of the first century Castro de San Lourenzo].* Continue over river bridge **[0.8** km] and LU-652 in **Cereixa [0.1** km].

2.9 km **Cereixa** *Rst. O Fogón left 200m.* Keep s/o past Igrexa S. Pedro and through the hamlet of **Rairos** onto a long and lovely stretch of track up steeply through woodland before dropping down over río Muiños and over canal and road into **Reigada** by *centro social & parque infantil.*

5.1 km **Reigada** No facilities. Continue through the village, turn *right* before river bridge, *under* main road, *over* irrigation channel along a narrow country lane closed in by high stone walls *corredoira* through shaded woodland into an area of low lying wetlands (path may be wet here) to finally cross the río Seco via *pasarela* with picnic area (right) into **Rioseco**, a suburb of Monforte de Lemos. Continue along r/ As Cruces and over the rail level crossing (see 'accommodation' for hotels by rail station right). Keep s/o r/ Ramón del Valle Inclán over a second level crossing and s/o down c/ Roberto Baamonde into r/ Doutor Teijeiro to arrive at plaza de España in the centre of the old town *casco histórico*. Continue down r/ do Comercio past **tourist office** *información turística* part of the wine cellar and interpretation centre *Centro do Viño Ribeira Sacra (well worth a visit)* to the heart of the historic quarter of Monforte de Lemos at the old medieval bridge A Ponte Vella.

2.9 km **Monforte de Lemos** *A Ponte Vella*. The historical centre of town and point over which pilgrims pass to reach Chantada on the next stage. The Hotel Puente Romano is located on the bridge (see photo) and popular cafe Cantón de Bailén which gets the last of the evening sun. The tourist office, frutería and outdoor sports shop are within 100 meters.

■ **Accommodation**: On the way into town, just as we pass over the *second* railway crossing, turn right at roundabout and continue alongside rail track for 1.1 km to the railway station *Estación:* ❶ **Hs Ohlala Galicia** *x5* €25 ☏ 982 400 010 r/ Rosalía de Castro, 24. ❷ *Hs* **Riosol** *x18* €38-48 ☏ 982 402 052 Plaza Estación, 5 ❸ *H***Condes de Lemos** *x30* €38-60 ☏ 982 400 319 *www.hotelcondesdelemos.com* Plaza Estación, 2. *Central:* ❹ *H*****Parador de Monforte de Lemos** *x50* €80+ ☏ 982 418 484 *www.parador.es* Plaza Luis de Góngora y Argote. ❺ *H*** & *Hs*** **Puente Romano** *x36* €20-40 ☏ 982 411 167 (Oscar) Paseo Malecón. ❻ *H*****Cardenal** *30* €60-75 ☏ 982 090 568 *www.hotelcardenal.es* c/Hortas, 36. ❼ *Hs* **MON ComeySueña** *x8* €28-50 ☏ 982 401 437 c/ Roberto Baamonde, 30. ❽ *H* **Miño** *x9* €25-35 ☏ 982 401 850 c/ Conde, 25. ❾ *H***Ribeira Sacra** *x17* €38-60 ☏ 982 411 706 *www.hotelribeirasacra.es* c/ Conde, 17. ❿ *Hs***Medievo** *x4* €35-45 ☏ 617 987 588 *www.hostalmedievo.com* on c/ Compañía, 21. *Otros:* ⓫ *Hs* **Duquesa** *x18* €25 ☏ 982 403 467 c/ Duquesa de Alba, 50 + 500m from Praza dos Escolapios. And last but not least: ⓬*Alb.* **Santiago-15** *Xunta.[50÷1]* €6 r/ Santiago 15 off Av. Ourense (N-120a) with 'rear' access /exit from the wide track to the rear of the building on Barro Cesar.

■ **Other facilities:** *Turismo* ☏ 982 404 715 r/ Comercio 10:00-14:00 16:30-20:00 closed Mondays. Wide choice of restaurants the majority conveniently located around the Plaza de España *café Chokolat* benefits from the evening

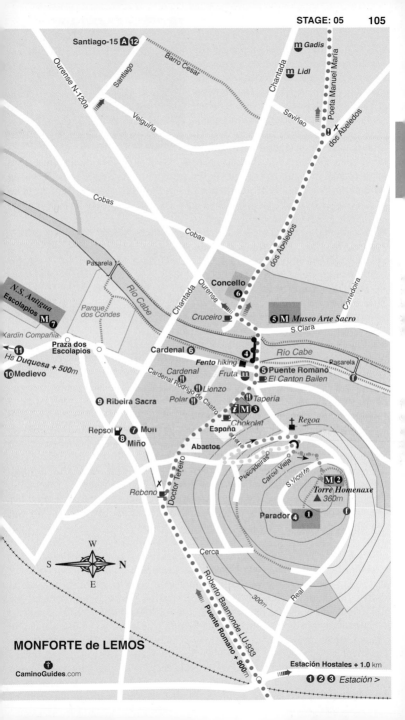

sun as does the *El Canton Bailen* adj. Puente Vieja. In between we find *Rst. Taperia* popular with pilgrims *menú del dia* adj. *Centro do Viño*. **Restaurants** spill out onto pedestrian r/ Cardenal (opp. Plaza España) incl: *Polar* (opens 06:45!) *Lienzo* and *Cardenal*. In r/ Hortas near the bridge is the **Outdoor shop** *Fento Monte y Rio* (hiking gear) Ⓒ 982 404 519. Opposite fresh fruit shop *Frutas*. You can hire a boat in the summer (June/Sept) from Quixós in Parque dos Condes and view the town from the river! And do make time to explore some of the historic buildings in the Casco Historico as follows:...

■ The monumental complex known *Monte de San Vicente del Pino* sits atop ❶ *El monasterio X-XVIc.* (with neo-classical Parador facade). ❷ *Torre del Homenaje XIII-XVc.* y *Palacio Condal XVI-XVIIc. (original palace of the Counts of Lemos).* It is well worth the effort to make it to the hilltop to take in the splendid views in all directions from the public area in

front of the Parador... or take the steps to the top of *Torre del Homenaje* and do homage to the view from there (entrance fee to tower and museum €1.50 open 11-14 / 17-20). The courtyard bar of the Parador (the original monastery) is rather formal. **Directions**: *(700m)* the hill is best approached via the broad steps in Plaza de España. Turn left into r/ Santo Domingo up by the formidable medieval walls past *Igrexa La Régoa* and take next sharp right under arch into r/ Pescaderías and s/o up left into r/ Carcel Vieja* *[Note the road s/o down right is a good alt. to take on the return as it goes through the ancient Jewish quarter via ruas Pescaderías* Fishmongers *Zapaterías* Cobblers *and Falagueira* Orators*].* Continue on r/ Carcel Vieja* and *up* left onto path that zigzags up to the top. Return the same way or via the old Jewish quarter (see town plan).

Just off Plaza de España on rua Commercio we find ❸ *Antigua Casa Consitorial XV1c. Centro do Vino y Interpretación da Ribeira Sacra.* Built in 1583 as the original town hall and medieval hospital and now houses the tourist office and excellent Wine Interpretation Centre. The entrance fee €2.50 includes a guided tour 11:30 /12:30 &17:30 /19:00 (English/Spanish) of viticulture since the Roman epoch and a taste of some of the wonderful grape varieties grown in the region D.O. (Denomination of Origin) especially the Mencía and Albariño. Next is ❹ **Puente Viejo** *XVIc. (medieval bridge built on earlier Roman foundations)* Note there are delightful walks along both banks of the river. Just over the bridge is ❺ *Museo de Arte Sacro de las Madres Clarisas XVIIc.* housing a valuable collection (one of the most important collections in Spain) of religious art and artefacts. The convent is home to the order of nuns *Franciscanas Descalzas.* A pleasant way to visit the other monuments and the town is to take the riverside path to the Parque dos Condes ❻ **Padres Escolapios** *XVI-XVIIc. (Colegio Nuestra Señora de la Antigua, often referred to as the 'Escorial de Galicia' as it houses important art works including several paintings by Goya).* The art works were gifted by the great art benefactor of Monforte de Lemos D. Pedro Fernández de Castro the 7th count of Lemos whose statue stands sentinel over the impressive Renaissance building reminiscent of San Marcos in León with its expansive

esplanade that encompasses the 'Park of the Counts'.

■ **Monforte de Lemos** beautifully located on the banks of the río Cabe, a tributary of the Sil. An historic town with Roman remains and a population of 20,000, the second largest in the province of Lugo. It serves an active industrial and administrative base with expanding tourism due to its status as 'capital' of the Ribeira Sacra wine growing region. The town has a camino association *www.caminodeinvierno.com* and the opening of a Xunta hostel in 2020 will no doubt increase the flow of pilgrims in the years ahead.

REFLECTIONS:

_____

_____

_____

_____

Ponte Vella & río Cabe

06 MONFORTE de Lemos – CHANTADA
Santiago—137.8 km

···············	--- ---	9.2	--- ---	30%
━━━━	--- ---	18.5	--- ---	60 %
▅▅▅▅	--- ---	<u>3.1</u>	--- ---	10 %
Total km		**30.8 km (19.1 ml)**		

▲ *equiv.* Ascent 1,850m (+9.3= **40.1 km!**)
Alto.m ▲ O Cerdeiro 630 m (2,065 ft)
< Ⓐ Ⓗ > *Vilariño* **16.1** *km* **+0.4** *km*
Diomondi **23.2** km

Our thoughts arrive one on top of another, like a steep mountain waterfall. Gradually [they] become like water in a deep, narrow gorge, then a great river slowly winding its way to the sea. Finally the mind becomes still like a placid ocean. Sogyal Rinpoche

❑ **Mystical Path:** Our journey along the camino reflects our changing state of mind. We start in a rush of excitement and sense of the physical adventure ahead. Arriving at 600 kph by air –300 kph with AVE we slow to a leisurely walking pace of just 3 kph. As the days pass we find our mind also slowing. A gap between our thoughts begins to open with an opportunity to linger in the void. The ego immediately tries to fill the gap but we can change the default setting to allow spaciousness to arise instead. We begin to learn from the Landscape Temple, content to be in present moment awareness.

❑ **Practical Path:** Another very long stage but Vilariño is a half way point with *off* route lodging at Torre Vilariño (+0.4 km) or Escairón (+3.4 km) the latter also has a bus service from Monforte. A new Xunta hostel in Diomondi makes another option to break the journey into 2 shorter stages. This is a sensational route as we drop down precipitously to cross the río Miño at Belesar before the steep climb up to Chantada, a charming town which no doubt will have its own pilgrim hostel in due course. Facilities *directly* en route are limited so take plenty of water and snacks for the journey ahead.

0.0 km **Ponte Vella** Cross the medieval bridge by Hostal Puente and turn left and next right by *Café Cruceiro* into ***Praza Campo de San Antonio*** past Casa do Concello into Rua dos Abeledos and veer s/o left into ***Rúa Poeta***

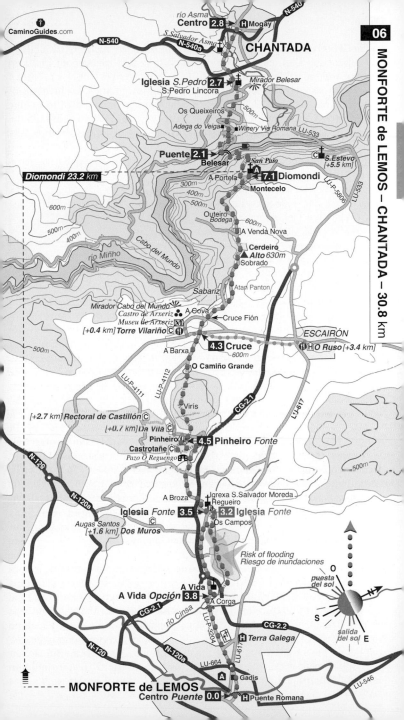

CaminoGuides.com

río Asma
Centro 2.8 H *Mogay*
S.Salvador Asma
N-540 N-540a
N-540 **CHANTADA**

Iglesia *S.Pedro* 2.7 *Mirador Belesar*
S.Pedro Lincora
Os Queixeiros
500m
Adega do Veiga *Winery Vía Romana* LU-533

Puente 2.1 C *S.Estevo*
Belesar *San Paio* [+5.5 km]
A Portela A **7.1 Diomondi**
Montecelo LU-P-5806

Diomondi 23.2 km
300m
400m
500m
Outeiro
600m Bodega
600m A *Venda Nova*
500m
400m
río Miño
Cabo del Mundo
Cerdeiro
▲ *Alto* 630m
Sobrado

Sabariz *Atan Panton*
Mirador Cabo del Mundo *A Cova*
Castro de Arxeriz ← *Cruce Fión*
Museu de Arxeriz M
[+0.4 km] **Torre Vilariño** C **ESCAIRÓN**
4.3 Cruce H *O Ruso* [+3.4 km]
A Barxa *600m*

O Camiño Grande
CG-2.1
LU-P-4111
LU-617
Viris
LU-P-4112
[+2.7 km] *Rectoral de Castillón* C
[+0.7 km] *Da Vila* C
Pinheiro C **4.5 Pinheiro** *Fonte*
Castrotañe C
Pazo O Reguengo

A Broza *Igrexa S.Salvador Moreda*
Iglesia *Fonte* 3.5 *Regueiro*
C **3.2 Iglesia** *Fonte*
Augas Santos *Os Campos*
[+1.6 km] *Dos Muros*

Risk of flooding
Riesgo de inundaciones

A Vida 4 *Opción* 3.8
A Corga
río Cinsa
CG-2.1 CG-2.2
N-120 H *Terra Galega*
N-120a LU-617
LU-664
LU-546

MONFORTE de LEMOS
Centro *Puente* 0.0 H *Puente Romana*
A *Gadis*

O puesta del sol
S
salida del sol *E*

Manuel María [!] [**0.6** km] *(easily missed in the early morning dark)*. Pass rear entrance to Lidl and Gadis hypermarkets to first roundabout [**0.4** km] *[Detour +400m •H°Terra Galega x16 €18-38 © 982 405 090 on LU 617]*. keep s/o to second roundabout (statue of pilgrim pointing in direction of Santiago) continue s/o LU-P-3204 a monotonous stretch of road to **bridge** [**2.5** km] (río Cinsa) into *A Corga / A Vida*. waymarks take us through the back of the village to option point [**0.3** km].

3.8 km A Vida *option* ▲▼ (photo>)

▼ For the original rural itinerary *(3.2 km by remote pathways -v- 3.6 km by road)* keep s/o to wide gravel track by the 30 kph sign (see photo>) *camino de servicio canal* also marked 'in bad state' *en mal estado!* Which is a fair description as the low lying track can become flooded in wet weather. Some of the original waymarks still exist but the tranquil woodland paths are somewhat overgrown. *[Only attempt in dry weather and if you are an experienced hiker. It is not feasible to monitor this route regularly so please email jb@caminoguides.com with any comments so these can be posted on the updates page to benefit pilgrims who follow]*. Continue for ½ km and turn left by mojón and under road **bridge** [**0.5** km]. The track is little used and overgrown here but you should be able to push through (s/o) to join a side track from left by **lake** [**1.1** km]. Keep s/o (lake on the left, dog kennel right) to low lying area liable to flood in wet weather to rejoin main waymarked route [**1.0** km] and continue to church of **San Salvador de Moreda** with *[F]*.

▲ For newly waymarked road route keep s/o past parish church over VG-2.1 **bypass** [**0.8** km] through parish of Moreda & **crossroads** [**1.7** km]. *[Detour+1.7 km •CR Casa dos Muros x10 €55 © 610 456 046 www.casadosmuros.com Outeiro, Paderne. Signposted Pantón left at crossroads and under road bridge visible ahead]*. Keep s/o at crossroads and turn **sharp right** [**0.3** km] onto dirt track into **Os Campos** [**0.2** km] where alt. route joins from the right. Continue through the parish of **Regueiro** to church of **San Salvador de Moreda** [**0.5** km] with fountain and rest area.

3.5 km Iglesia *San Salvador de Moreda* [F] foot-pump operated. Rejoin road through **A Broza** [**1.6** km] and s/o over crossroads and over río Carabelos to pass the gates of the impressive **Pazo de O Reguengo** [**0.8** km]. We now turn **left** [**0.3** km] onto woodland path around the side of the Pazo and into the tiny hamlet of **Castrotañe** [**0.7** km] population 2! Resident Penelope Anderton © 677 120 321 has adj.'La Casita' to let *www.galiciaholidayrentals.com* but no longer takes one night stays. Continue along a beautiful stretch of woodland path with stone walls either side, a classic *corredoira* into the hamlet of **Piñeiro** [**1.1** km].

4.5 km **Piñeiro** *[F]* fountain with stone bench seat. Turn left at T-junction and imm. **right [0.1 km]** back onto track *or [Detour s/o +700m to •CR **Da Vila** €40 © 676 335 565 www.casaruraldavila. com lovely manor house set in peaceful gardens, dinner €12. Or 2.0 km beyond to the sumptuous •Hotel & Rst. **Rectoral de Castillón** www.rectoraldecastillon. com from €58 accessed down a maze of*

tree-lined country lanes past San Vicente and Igrexa Santiago de Castillón]. Continue up track through minuscule hamlets of *Outeiriño, Virís* and over equally tiny stream *Rego de Penaalda* back onto the asphalt lane at *O Camiño Grande* up to join road in **A Barxa [3.7 km]**. Continue by road to next major crossroads **[0.5 km]**.

4.3 km **Cruce** *option* Several options here ❶ keep s/o waymarked route

❷ *Detour left +0.4 km to cafe and lodging at **Torre Vilariñho** Rst.•CR **Torre Vilariño** x10 €50 (pilgrim price €15+ pp when sharing) Menú €10 © 982 452 260 www.torrevilarino.com pleasant cafe and casa rural. Return same way or via **Museo Etnográfico de Arxeriz** [400m] turn up right at next **crossroads** [500m]* and rejoin waymarked route in **Fión** [200m].*

additional detour +400m to **Cabo do Mundo viewpoint (pleasant woodland walk but not recommended as trees now take away the view!).*

❸ *Detour right +3.4 km to all facilities incl. bus connections in **Escairón**. Also •H** **O Ruso** €37 © 982 452 134 Praza de España. If walking this latter option take the first turn right 200m and keep s/o and over CG-2.1 into Escairón on quiet road parallel to the main LU-P-4102 – see map].*

❶ Keep s/o at crossroads and s/o through A Cova/ Fontela/ **Fión [0.4 km]** (where route from Torre Vilariño joins from left). The next long stretch of asphalt road has no facilities but is relieved by occasional glimpses of the mighty Miño and Cape of the World *Cabo do Mundo* to our left (West). Continue through Sobrado and **Cerdeiro [3.4 km]** which is our high point of the day at 630m. Shortly after we enter Vendanova with Chantada just visible in the distance. We now start a gentle descent down past Bodega (left) and Montecelo and its ancient cruceiro (right) to **Diomondi [3.3 km]**.

7.1 km **Diomondi** *Igrexa* San Paio de Diomondi *XIIc*. well preserved stone carvings portraying animals and mystical beasts so characteristic of 12th

century Romanesque architecture (see west entrance door frieze above).

● *Alb.* **Diomondi** *Xunta.[33÷4]* €8. Historic building renovated in 2020 with all modern facilities incl. kitchen. A welcome addition to the Xunta network as this stage to Chantada had no lodging directly en route until this former bishops palace was turned into a pilgrim hostel (parish of O Saviñao).

*[Originally a summer residence of the Bishops of Lugo in the Middle Ages then a rectory and now a pilgrims hostel! In a masterful stroke the Xunta has preserved an historic building and created a much needed albergue in an ideal location that carves this challenging stage into two very 'doable' sections. While there are only 8.0 km to Chantada it includes a very steep descent **down** to the Belesar valley floor of 610m and equally steep climb **back up** giving an additional effort of 3.1 km equivalent 11.1 km to the town centre. Chantada is a pleasant place to catch up and has good facilities – although currently no dedicated hostel].*

We now start the steep zigzag descent down to cross the Miñho in Belesar. [!] Take care, especially in wet conditions on the cobblestone sections *part of the original Roman Via XVIII.* Turn down by shelter and 100 km mark! signposted **A Portela** onto a series of delightful woodland pathways that open up with splendid views over the Miñho valley and its steep sided wine

groves to emerge onto road by the bridge in Belesar:

2.1 km **Belesar** *puente* *[F]* (See photo opposite) *[+200m right Abaceria O Batuxo ℂ 610 056 774 (occasional opening hours) by Club Fluvial with summer boat trips].* Cross the bridge and take the path for one of the steepest and most spectacular climbs of the whole Winter route but each step is accompanied by breathtaking (literally and metaphorically) views over the river with its banks strewn with vineyards. Turn right along road to A Ermida and ***Bodegas Via Romana*** **[1.4** km] *(yes the measurement is correct is just seems further)* where you can sample the local wines or gastronomy in its exclusive restaurant opposite *Meson e Adega Do Veiga* © 657 805 731 *(occasional opening hours).* Continue up and veer off right **[0.2** km] onto path down over stepping stones by old mill building (ruin) and up into **OS Queixeiros [0.5** km]. [!] Watch out for indistinct waymark up steep stone access ramp by house with large wooden veranda and back onto track. Towards the top our route finally levels out through *A Devesa* as we enter **Lincora [0.6** km].

2.7 km **Lincora** *Igrexa San Pedro* No facilities *(a planned hostel did not materialise). The **Miradoiro de Líncora** is 900m off route but offers no addition to the views we have already enjoyed].* Continue along LU-P-1804 *under* the **N-540 [1.5** km] to **Asma [0.5** km] *[50m left **Igrexa y monasterio San Salvador de Asma** IXc. (9th century!) Romanesque church with view over Chantada].* We now enter the suburbs of Chantada over río Asma

by *pasarela* and follow the shaded promenade past *bar Pio Lindo* (right) and *Bar No Río* (left) by riverside and Parque do Alameda *[F]*. Keep s/o up the colonnaded r/ do Dous de Maio, past *Rst. Lucus* (see photo>) to municipal library *Biblioteca Pública* and helpful tourist office **Turismo** Ⓒ 982 441 752 on **Praza do Mercado [0.5 km]**. The heart of the old town *(an ideal location for a pilgrim hostel! Anyone listening?)* To head for the bars & limited lodging keep s/o into r/ Comercio *(turn right into Trovador Xan Requeixo for Hotel Mogay just before ✚ Farmacia...Sampayo)* s/o over main road *Av. Monforte* onto pedestrian r/ de Leonardo Rodríguez with range of *cafés* & *restaurants* up to Plaza Santa Ana, the main *paseo* of town **[0.3** km] *cafés Os Angeles* & *Parada* with Hostal Gamallo +250m

2.8 km Chantada *centro Plaza Santa Ana*.

■ **Lodging**: currently limited but pressure for an albergue is gathering momentum (check updates page or the tourist office). ❶ *H*****Mogay** *x29* €44-55 Ⓒ 982 440 847 *www.mogay.com* central located on Antonio Lorenzana. ❷*P* **Yoel** *x6* €17-25 Ⓒ 982 440 294 above *discoteca!* Ramón y Cajal, 10 (Av. de Lugo). ❸ *Hs* **Gamallo** *x24* €15 (special pilgrim price) €20-40 Ⓒ 982 440 833 (Luis) top end of town on c/ Julio Camba,1. ❹ *H*** **Las Delicias** *x20* €24-38 Ⓒ 982 441 701 **+ 1.4** km from town centre on the main road Lugo-Ourense.

■ **Chantada Town**: The geographical centre of Galicia with population of 8,000 (15,000 in the year 1900). Noted for its range of Romanesque buildings and San Salvador de Asma founded in the 9th century. Of particular charm are the arcaded streets *soportales* with their noble houses dating from the 16th century. **Turismo** Praza do Mercado (see photo>) Ⓒ 982 441 752

Daily 10:00-14:00–16:00-20:00. Sat 11:00–14:00 Closed Sun & Mon.

■ **Other Facilities**: Range of restaurants with *menús* include: *Rst. Lucus* with rear terrace overlooking the river. *Rst. A Faragulla* gourmet menu with rear access from/to Mogay and nearby the trendy *bar Meigas* and several popular bars around pedestrian r/ de Leonardo Rodríguez. If *pulpo* is your thing *pulpería Os Pendellos* up on Parque Campo da Feira is recommended. If you need **hiking gear** try *Jamex* c/ Luciano Travadelo, 4 (start of pedestrian street). **Laundry** LavraXpress 08:00-22:00 r/ das Chedas 8 by Plaza de Galicia.

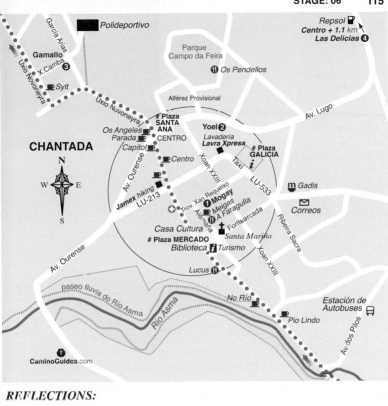

REFLECTIONS:

07 CHANTADA – RODEIRO
Santiago—107 km

▓▓▓▓▓▓	--- ---	16.0 --- ---	*60%*
▬▬▬▬	--- ---	10.8 --- ---	*40%*
▬▬▬▬	--- ---	<u>0.0</u> --- ---	*0%*
Total km		**26.8** km (16.7 ml)	

equiv. ◢ Ascent 1,410 m (+7.1=**33.9** km)

Alto.m ▲ Monte Faro 1,190 m (3,905 ft)

< Ⓐ Ⓗ > *Vilaseco 5.8 km +0.8 / Penasillás 8.0 km +3.8 km*

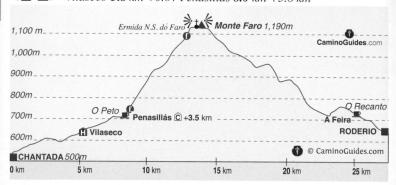

> *Never measure the height of a mountain until you reach the top. Then you will see how low it was... The longest journey is the journey inwards.*
>
> Dag Hammerskjold

❏ **Mystical Path:** The caminos offer one of the most potent forces for positive change in our war-torn world. Representatives from every nation on earth have walked its pathways as an act of faith and reconciliation. The journey is both a walk in nature and a journey of soul, *The way within the way without.* Dag Hammarskjöld, UN Secretary-General and Nobel Peace Prize recipient reminds us that, *the pursuit of peace, with all its trials and errors, can never be relaxed nor abandoned.* Our sacred contract is always some form of bringing more love into the world. Let's support each other in fulfilling that great pursuit and heed the words of the great naturalist John Muir, *The mountain is calling, and I must go.*

❏ **Practical Path:** Don't be alarmed! The 2D contour image above is somewhat deceiving; the route winds itself *around* Monte Faro rather than straight up. A glorious 60% is on earth tracks including the section parallel to the CG-21 which is not even visible from the tree-lined path. And yes, this is a demanding stage as it reaches the highest point on the entire Camino Invierno at 1,190m (close on 4,000 ft). Facilities en route are very limited and the cafés at Penasillás and A Feira may not be open when you pass. So take plenty of water and energy snacks for the day ahead. There is an 'alternative road route' via Mouricios if the weather is bad but this misses the spectacular views and historic pilgrim site of Monte Faro itself.

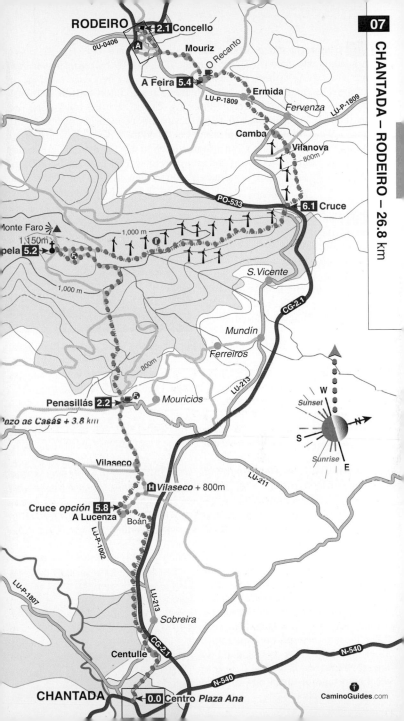

RODEIRO

0U-0406

A ← **2.1** Concello

Mouriz

O Recanto

A Feira ← **5.4**

LU-P-1809

Ermida

Fervenza

LU-P-1809

Camba

Vilanova

800m

PO-533

6.1 Cruce

Monte Faro ▲

1,150m

pela → **5.2**

1,000 m

1,000 m

S.Vicente

CG-2.1

Mundín

800m

Ferreiros

LU-213

Mouricios

Penasillás 2.2

azo as Casas + 3.8 km

Vilaseco

H *Vilaseco* + 800m

LU-211

Cruce *opción* **5.8**
A Lucenza

Boán

LU-P-1002

W

Sunset

S

N

Sunrise

E

LU-P-1807

Sobreira

LU-213

CG-2.1

Centulle

N-540

N-540

CHANTADA ← **0.0** Centro *Plaza Ana*

CaminoGuides.com

0.0 km Chantada *Plaza Santa Ana* from the 'square' *café Parada opens early* head up unnamed r/ Alférez Banante /LU-P-1809 by *pasteleria Miguel* and up past *café Sylt* (those staying at *Hs Gamallo* join here) and continue up out of town keeping s/o by roadside **shrine [1.0** km] into **Centulle [0.3** km]. We now veer right and turn right along LU-213 to take the track (left) just *before* the CG-2.1 **underpass [0.4** km] (easily missed in the darkness of early morning). We continue along a pleasant tree-lined track parallel to the CG-2.1 and turn off left into Boán to join a short stretch of asphalt road to Crossroads hamlet of **A Lucenza [3.9** km] and continue to second crossroads **[0.2** km] where the waymarked route continues s/o along track. At this point there is an option.

5.8 km Cruce *option A Lucenza* ▲ *Detour: +800m •H**Vilaseco* (photo>) *x12* €50 Manuel © 982 587 160 www.hotelvilaseco.es +●*Alb. Priv. [24÷2]* €16. If you need a break or plan overnighting here turn right and continue along quiet country lane when the hotel/Albergue comes shortly into view.

▲ At option point outside *A Lucenza* keep s/o along track and continue into:

2.2 km Penasillás *Tarberno O Peto. [F.]* if the café is closed when you pass (usually opens around 9:00) there is a fonte (signposted) 'around the back'. Traditional rural village with stone *capela* in the central green.

▲ *[Detour: +3.7 km •Pazo as Casas x10* €45-55 © 982 446 566 www. pazoascasas.es in San Pedro de Viana – free pick-up from Penasillás].

Alternative low level Road Route: via Mouricios, Ferreiros, Mundín & San Vincente. In poor visibility or those otherwise not wishing to scale Monte Faro it's possible to skirt around the side of the mountain via quiet country lanes, all by asphalt. Rejoin main waymarked route where it crosses the CG-2.1. It is 1.5 km shorter but misses the steep climb... and splendid views!

Keep s/o out of Penasillás where the asphalt quickly gives way to a stone and gravel track, partly shaded. We pass stone **monolith [2.6** km] with engraving of poem by Pablo Rubén Eyre at which point we rejoin the asphalt road to *[F.]* (right) **[2.2** km]. Take the stone steps opposite, up a short but steep grass path flanked by the stone crosses of the Via Crucis to the **hermitage of our Lady of Faro [0.4** km]. (see photo>).

`5.2 km` **Ermida de Nosa Señora do Faro** *alto*. This is our high point of this stage and the whole of the Camino Invierno at 1,150m. We have a spectacular vista in all directions. A 'viewing gallery' 400m further on by the look out tower visible ahead adds little to the panorama from the wide plateau in front of the hermitage. The

current building was erected in the twelfth century although this has been a place of strong religious veneration for many centuries. Thousands of pilgrims attend here every September 8th. In front of the hermitage is a stone cross depicting Adam and Eve.

Waymarks now bring us back down an access road onto a gravel track past the *[F.]* (that we passed on the way up, now down to our right) and along the giant windmills either side of our path *Parque Eólico Monte Cabeza* and, while this is a heavily forested area, the trees offer little shade because of the wide path and its orientation. We pass the wooden steps up to the **Fonte dos Meniños [3.2 km]** *[site of a legendary cure for children]* all the way down to cross the main road **PO-533 [2.9 km]**.

`6.1 km` **Cruce** *PO-533* Continue via wide track to enter hamlet of **Vilanova [1.7 km]** we continue through **Vilanova de Camba** *Igrexa de San Xoán XIIc.* and adj. 15th century Pazo and over the main road into **A Feira [3.7 km]**.

`5.4 km` **A Feira** *Bar O Recanto*. Small village with one bar / Restaurant. We now make our way through **Mouriz** to join main road LU P 1809 on the outskirts of **Rodeiro**. [Note option **A** to leave the waymarked route just after passing the 50 kph sign to go direct to *albergue* **Carpinteiras** at the 'top' of town (see town map for this option) or **B** take the next turn left to go direct to *Pensión* **O Guerra** at the central crossroads or **C** follow the waymarks s/o alongside the main road parallel to *rego da Costa de Saíme* and wetlands to the town hall **Concello** and **Puente** at the lower end of town.

`2.1 km` **Rodeiro** *Concello Puente* café *Estraloxo* adjoining the bridge over the río Rodeiro which we pass over to continue on towards Lalín.

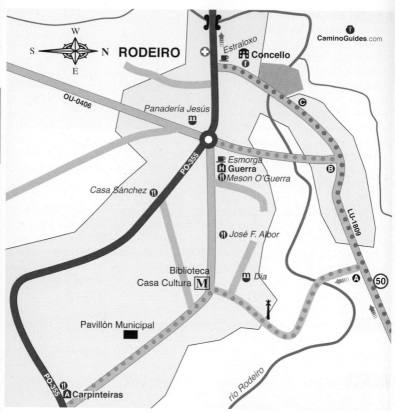

RODEIRO: resident population of 2,500 (8,000 in 1950) with welcoming Albergue / Hostal at the top end of town (+0.6 km from the Concello). ●*Alb. Priv.[24÷2] [28÷3]* •**Carpinteiras** €12 +*14* €22-34 ℭ 986 790 196 (Luis) on Av. Lalín (PO-533). Pilgrim menú, breakfast €3 all facilities including washing and drying equipment. Descending towards the

bridge over the rio Rodeiro we pass the library *biblioteca* and come to the central roundabout *rotonda* with monument of a Wheel *monumento a la Rueda* (possible derivation of the name Rodeiro) and *Rst.•Pensión* **O Guerra** *x14* €30+ ℭ 986 790 061 with new annex adj. *Bar Esmorga*. On the opposite side of the rotonda is *Panadería Jesús* which bakes bread for the Spanish Royal family and sends it to the palace in Madrid and has done so, from this humble bakery, for many decades. Buy some and taste the bread of kings! Market day is Thursday.

REFLECTIONS:

Early morning mist leaving Chantada

08 RODEIRO – LALÍN – A LAXE

Santiago—80.2 km

▪▪▪▪▪▪▪▪▪▪▪	--- ---	16.3	--- ---	60%
▬▬▬▬▬	--- ---	11.2	--- ---	40%
▬▬▬	--- ---	<u>0.0</u>	--- ---	0%
Total km		**28.5**km (17.6 ml)		

equiv.
Ascent 1,390m (+6.9=**35.2** km)
Alto.*m* ▲ Monte Faro 690 m (2,260 ft)
< **A** **H** > Lalín **22.3** km

I hear the crowing cock / I hear the note / Of lark and linnet / and from every page / Rise odors of ploughed field or flowery mead. Longfellow on Chaucer

❑ **Mystical Path:** The tale of the Miller, the Nun, the Knight, the Merchant... How our stories intertwine with one another. And at the end of this stage we join with pilgrims coming along the camino Sanabrés and our soul family suddenly becomes extended, more stories are added to the collection. The true badge of the pilgrim is not a cockle shell but a loving heart and kindly ear. When we meet the 'other' we look into a mirror and see our own reflection; a smiley face or scowling countenance. Will we stay awake today and hear the call of the lark... and our brother/sister. *Before the rooster crows today, you will deny three times that you know me. Luke 22:34.*

❑ **Practical Path:** Today has the same cumulative height gain as yesterday. But unlike one straight hike up Monte Faro today we gently undulate along the 600m contour line that follows the río Arnego, tributary of the Ulla, to A Ponte de Pedroso. There are NO facilities until we reach Lalín excepting a water font at Pedroso. Bring plenty of water and snacks for this isolated day. The 'official' route through Lalín town follows a maze of twists and turns; not all clearly waymarked. A straightforward alternative is provided and while it only saves 600m in distance it could save time in needless wandering! The remainder of the route to A Laxe, where it rejoins the route from Ourense, starts off alongside the lovely riverside park *parque fluvial* before making its way through Lalín's busy industrial park. If you are staying in Lalín there is a variety of lodging including a private albergue (see town plan).

0.0 km **Rodeiro** *Concello Puente café Estraloxo* (if you are coming from *albergue Carpinteiras* add 0.8 km). Keep s/o over the río Rodeiro past *Meroil gaolinera* and onto service road that runs alongside the PO-533 (Lalín – Monforte) over río Arnego and turn right> opposite Cogal factory.

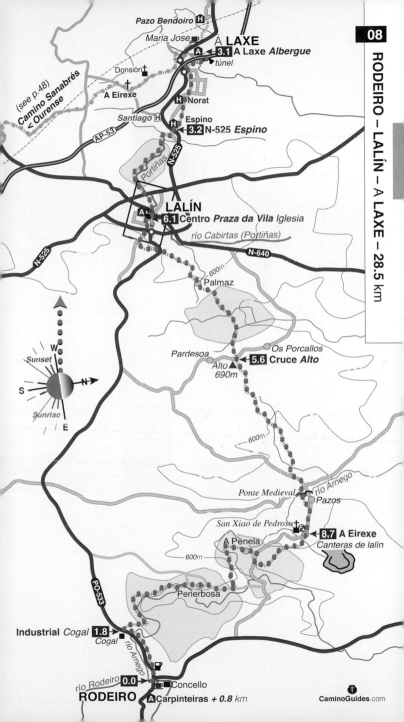

Pazo Bendoiro Ⓗ

Maria Jose

A **LAXE**

Ⓐ **3.1** *A Laxe Albergue*

→ *túnel*

Donsión †

A Eirexe

† *Santiago* Ⓗ

Ⓗ *Norat*

Ⓗ *Espino*

3.2 N-525 *Espino*

(see p.48)

Camino Sanabrés < Ourense

AP-53

Portiñas

N-525

Ⓐ **LALÍN**

6.1 Centro *Praza da Vila Iglesia*

río Cabirtas (Portiñas)

N-525

N-640

Palmaz

600m

Pardesoa ○ *Os Porcallos*

▲ *Alto* **5.6** Cruce *Alto*

690m

600m

Ponte Medieval ○ río Arnego

○ *Pazos*

San Xiao de Pedroso †

8.7 A Eirexe

Canteras de lalín

A Penela

600m

Penerbosa

PO-533

Industrial *Cogal* **1.8**

Cogal

río Arnego

río Rodeiro **0.0**

■ *Concello*

RODEIRO

Ⓐ *Carpinteiras + 0.8 km*

1.8 km PO-533 *Cogal* Turn right opp. Cogal factory and keep s/o where the asphalt gives way to a delightful track by the rio Arnego with silver birch and other deciduous trees lining our route. We cross the river several times before entering **Penerbrosa [3.4 km]** (no services) and continue through **A Penela [2.8 km]** with its bizarre 'mausoleum' erected to commemorate a victory in a lawsuit over... a watercourse! But no water-font here. Shortly afterwards we drop down towards Eirexe de Pedroso where the open cast granite quarry opens up directly ahead (photo>). We pass the

access road to the quarry and pass a classic wayside cross *cruceiro* (see photo opposite) to enter **Eirexe [2.5 km]**.

8.7 km Eirexe de Pedroso remote hamlet with church dedicated to St. John *Igrexa de San Xiao de Pedroso* and adj. cemetery where, unusually, the burial niches open directly onto the street. At the entrance to the church is a welcome *[F]*. No other facilities. We continue passing the tiny hamlets of Pazos and Laxas and into **A Ponte de Pedroso [1.4 km]** over the 12th century medieval bridge with single stone arch where we cross the Arnego River for the last time. We continue back onto track to our high point of this stage at **crossroads [4.2 km]**.

5.6 km Cruce *alto* keep s/o over road along a long stretch of gravel track through **Palmaz [3.1 km]** and then we have sections of asphalt and track (well signposted) before entering the suburbs of upper Lalín. Turn right at crossroads and follow the lane between the modern houses (left) and woodland (right) down along Rúa do Cruceiro and keep s/o over the **ring road** *circunvalación* **[1.9 km]** *Rolda Leste* past fine stone cross *cruceiro* (left) to the Romanesque church **Igrexa de San Martiño** *de Lalín de Arriba* **[0.1 km]** and **option**. At this point the waymarked route takes a wide and somewhat illogical loop through modern suburbs *up* to the left. The route is poorly waymarked and has to compete with other signs of a busy city and so it is easy to get lost in the maze of streets.

Alternative direct route through Lalín: At **Igrexa de San Martiño** turn right down Rua Monte Faro (church on our left) and turn left along the busy PO-533 **[50**m]. This brings us directly into **Praza da Vila [300**m]. Total 350m -v- 450 km.

To continue on the waymarked route turn up left by church through the Cuartel Garda Civil and turn right down Rua Garda Civil into Rua Calzada to the centre of Lalín in **Praza da Vila [1.0 km]**.

6.1 km Centro Lalín *Praza da Vila* Igrexa N.S. das Dores *café A Barra.*

Several cafés surround the pedestrian square *La Garota* and *Rst. Currás*. Take time to orienate before proceeding. If you are staying in Lalín the albergue is only 250m away accessed through the Colon galleries, key with owner of Casa do Gato. Alternative lodging is widespread as follows:

Central: ❶*Alb.* **Lalín** *Priv.[20÷3]* €10 ✆ 610 207 992 c/ Observatorio, 8-2° via Galerias Colon (see photo >) *(key with Emiliano Gargía Casa do Gato r/ Ramon Aller 5).* The other main lodging is down towards r/ da Ponte and rio Cabirtas around the handsome statue of the horses (see photo). ❷ *Rst.P*** **Casa Mouriño** *x3* €30 ✆ 986 780 073. ❸ *H*** **El Palacio** *x34* www.hotelelpalacio.es €30-35 ✆ 986 780 000 c/ Matemático Rodríguez, 10 opp. ❹ *Rst./Hs* **As Vilas** €20 ✆ 986 780 140 r/ do Areal, 4 adj. ❺ *P** **Las Palmeras** *x16* €19-35 ✆ 986 780 222. *Exiting on N-525:* ❻ *H**** **Pontiñas** *x24-*€30-45 ✆ 986 787 147 www.hotelpontinas.com r/ da Ponte, 82. ❼ *Hs** **Caracas** *x8* €20-45 ✆ 680 176 205 c/ Corredoira, 32. ❽ *H**** **Villanueva** *x32* €30-45 ✆ 986 780 344 www.hotelvillanueva.com c/ Corredoira, 84.

We continue to A Laxe where we join the route from Ourense by continuing down the pedestrianised section of r/ Monte Faro and at the junction of c/ Principal at which point we find the centre of Galicia! *Kilometro Cero de Galicia.* Keep s/o over calle Principal into c/ Colón past the brass pig, a monument to the pork products of the area *Monumento ao Porco* and into Praza de Torre with statue of aviator *Estatua de Joaquín Loriga* (right).

Keep s/o down r/ Colón into r/ Praza Concello and finally into r/ do Regueiriño with a series of mini roundabouts and car park leading to the delightful **Paseo Fluvial del Río Pontiñas** [0.5 km] which we join and continue *under* the N-525. The riverside track continues for another 2½ kilometres over *pasarela* [2.4 km] up and *over* [!] **N-525** [0.3 km]

3.2 km N-525 Espino *Praza da Vila* •*H** **Naval do Espiño** *x30* €30-35 ✆

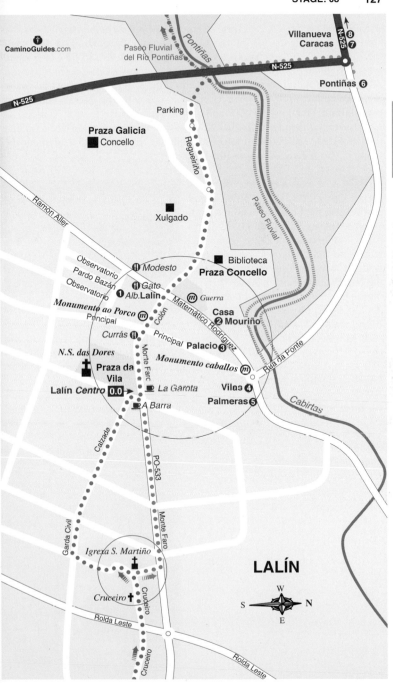

CaminoGuides.com

Paseo Fluvial del Río Pontiñas

Pontiñas

Villanueva Caracas **8 7**

N-525

N-525

Pontiñas 6

Parking

N-525

Praza Galicia
Concello

Regueiriño

Paseo Fluvial

Xulgado

Biblioteca
Praza Concello

Observatorio
Pardo Bazán
Observatorio

Modesto
Gato
1 Alb. Lalín
Matemático Rodríguez
Guerra

Monumento ao Porco
Principal

Colón

Casa
2 Mouriño

Ramón Aller

Currás

Principal

Palacio 3

Monte Faro

N.S. das Dores

Praza da Vila

Monumento caballos

Rúa da Ponte

Lalín *Centro* **0.0**

La Garota

Vilas 4

Palmeras 5

A Barra

Cabirtas

Calzada

PO-533

Monte Faro

Garda Civil

Igrexa S. Martiño

LALÍN

W
S · N
E

Cruceiro

Cruceiro

Rolda Leste

Cruceiro

Rolda Leste

986 787 064 on Espiño, 29. *[Note adjacent Hs Camino de Santiago currently closed]*. Continue to rear of the O Espiño into **Bergazos [1.2** km] past the luxury •*H*****& *Spa* **Torre do Deza** *x50* €55-95 © 986 787 666 *www.torredodezahotel.com* at the outskirts of the business park *parque empresarial*. A short stretch of grass track brings us into the Lalín's busy industrial estate *polígono industrial* which we skirt back down to the N-525 and major **roundabout [1.1** km] (N-525 and AP-53 Autoestrada Central Galicia) at *Construcións Taboada y Ramos S.L.* We now take the gravel service road that runs alongside (below) the motorway and take the *tunél* **[0.5** km] under the motorway to *A Laxe albergue* **[0.3** km].

3.1 km A **Laxe** *Bendoiro* ●*Alb.* A **Laxe** *Xunta.[30÷2]* €8. This is the point where the Camino Sanabrés from Ourense meets the Camino Invierno from Ponferrada. Nothing much to mark the spot beyond the albergue wedged between the motorway and the N-525 and softened, somewhat, by the gently flowing waters of the rego de Laxe dos Mosqueiros. *Bar / Rst.*

Maria José [+0.4 km] on the N-525 offers the only local services. Those seeking a luxury end to the Winter route can stay at the beautiful hotel and spa •*H******Pazo de Bendoiro** *[+1.4 km – 150m off route] x10* €65+ © 986 794 289 *www.pazodebendoiro.com* with good restaurant and swimming pool on Lugar de Bendoiro Abaixo.

Go to page 52 for the next stage from A Laxe to Ponte Ulla and the final stage into **Santiago de Compostela**.

Photo>
Path into Santiago: Rúa de Sar
The Sanabrés 'Monte do Gozo'

REFLECTIONS:

_____
_____
_____
_____
_____
_____
_____
_____
_____
_____
_____
_____
_____
_____
_____
_____
_____
_____
_____
_____
_____
_____
_____
_____

Path into A Eirexe:

You are encouraged to join your local confraternity (see list opposite) who may provide an official pilgrim passport *Credencial do Peregrino*. This is essential if you intend to apply for a Compostela in Santiago. You can also obtain an official *credencial* at the commencement of your journey or in major towns and cities en route (at the cathedrals or local association offices). Apart from establishing your pilgrim status they are necessary when staying in municipal and association hostels and they make an interesting record of your travels. A pilgrim stamp *sello* can readily be obtained from churches, hostels, hotels etc.

To be awarded the *Compostela* ❶ You need to have made the pilgrimage for religious reasons or for a similar motivation such as a vow. ❷ You need to have walked the last 100 kms or cycled the last 200 kms and to have collected at least two stamps *sellos* each day on your *credencial* as proof. The 'two stamp' rule only applies to the last stages within Galicia to ensure only those walking (or cycling) the route without any backup support or transport will receive a *Compostela.* Those who do not accept a spiritual motivation for their journeying can obtain a certificate (€3) recording the distance they have walked *Certificado de Distancia*.

Stay in Touch: The evolution of human consciousness is gathering apace. One manifestation of this is the increasing interest in taking time out to go on pilgrimage and nowhere is this more apparent than along the camino where facilities struggle to keep up with demand. Information garnered in one month may be out of date the next as old hostels close and new ones open up. Paths are realigned to make way for new motorways and budget airlines suddenly announce new routes. Whilst great care has been taken in gathering the information for this guide it also requires feedback from pilgrims who have recently walked the route to enable it to stay fresh and relevant to those who will follow on after us. Your comments and suggestions will be gratefully received and used to provide up-to-date advice on the 'updates' page on *www.caminoguides.com* so if you would like to offer something back to the camino or simply stay in touch please e-mail: *jb@caminoguides.com*

NEXT STEPS?...

The official literature for the last Compostelan jubilee year *año jubilar compostelana* stated boldly on the front cover, 'A Road with an END' *Camino que tiene META*. That may be so – but it is not the end of the road. Before you leave this corner of the earth why not visit the end of it *Finis Terra*: "… **Finisterre** is one of the great hidden treasures amongst the many Caminos de Santiago. Only a small proportion of pilgrims arriving at Santiago continue *by foot* to the end of the road. The way to Finisterre truly follows *the road less travelled* and *that* may make all the difference. We need to search out the waymarks to the source of our own inner knowing. The light, while obscured, lies hidden in our memory – it is no coincidence that the path to Finisterre ends at the altar to the sun *Ara Solis* and a lighthouse." From *A Pilgrim's Guide to the Camino Finisterre.*

PILGRIM ASSOCIATIONS:
UK: Confraternity of St. James +44 [0]2079 289 988 *www.csj.org.uk* the pre-eminent site in English with online bookshop.
IRELAND: Camino Society Ireland. Based in Dublin: *www.caminosociety.ie*
U.S.A. American Pilgrims on the Camino. *www.americanpilgrims.com*
CANADA: Canadian Company of Pilgrims Canada. *www.santiago.ca*
SOUTH AFRICA: Confraternity of St. James of SA *www.csjofsa.za.org*
AUSTRALIA: Australian Friends of the Camino *www.afotc.org*

SANTIAGO:
Pilgrim Office *www.oficinadelperegrino.com/en*
Son do Camiño 'discover more...' *www.sondocamino.com*
Tourism: *www.santiagoturismo.com*
Luggage storage & transfer / forum & meeting space *www.casaivar.com*
Backpack storage & local tours *www.pilgrim.es* Rúa Nova, 7 (adj. cathedral)

PILGRIM WEBSITES: (in English) loosely connected with the Way of St. James or with the theme of pilgrimage that you may find helpful.

Camino News: Largest online camino forum *www.caminodesantiago.me*
Walk Your Way: *www.urcamino.com*
Alternatives of St. James: *www.alternatives.org.uk* Exploration of ways of living that honour all spiritual traditions. Based at St. James Church, London.
The British Pilgrimage Trust: *www.britishpilgrimage.org*
Gatekeeper Trust pilgrimage & planetary healing *www.gatekeeper.org.uk*
Findhorn Foundation personal & planetary transformation *www.findhorn.org*
Lucis Trust spiritual education & World Goodwill *www.lucistrust.org*
Paulo Coelho reflections from author of The Pilgrimage *paulocoelhoblog.com*
Peace Pilgrim Her life and work *www.peacepilgrim.com*
The Quest A Guide to the Spiritual Journey *www.thequest.org.uk*
Pilgrimage in the Internet Age: *www.walkingtopresence.com*

ALBERGUE, HOSTAL AND HOTEL BOOKING SITES:
List of albergues open in Winter: *www.aprinca.com/alberguesinvierno/*
Private Network* Red de Albergues: *www.alberguescamino.com*
Albergues: *www.onlypilgrims.com*
Hostals: *www.hostelworld.com*
Paradores: *www.paradores.es*
Hotels: *www.booking.com*
B&Bs: *www.airbnb*
Christian Hospitality Network: *http://en.ephatta.com*

PILGRIM AND BACKPACK TRANSFERS / STORES:
Spanish Postal Service: *http://www.elcaminoconcorreos.com/en/*
General Listing: *www.amawalker.blogspot.co.uk*
All routes: (incl. Sanabrés from Ourense) *www.pilbeo.com/en*
Also: *www.caminofacil.net*

BIBLIOGRAPHY: Some reading with waymarks to the inner path include:

A Course In Miracles (A.C.I.M.) *Text, Workbook for Students and Manual for Teachers*. Foundation for Inner Peace.

A Return to Love *Reflections on A Course in Miracles*. Marianne Williamson. HarperCollins

Anam Cara *Spiritual wisdom from the Celtic world,* John O'Donohue. Bantam.

A New Earth *Awakening to Your Life's Purpose*, Eckhart Tolle. Penguin

A Brief History of Everything *Integrating the partial visions of specialists into a new understanding of the meaning and significance of life*, Ken Wilber.

Care of the Soul *How to add depth and meaning to your everyday life,* Thomas Moore. Piatkus

Conversations with God Neale Donald Walsch. Hodder & Stoughton

From the Holy Mountain *A Journey in the Shadow of Byzantium*, William Dalrymple. Flamingo

Going Home *Jesus and Buddha as brothers*, Thich Nhat Hanh. Rider Books

Loving What Is *Four Questions That Can Change Your Life*, Byron Katie. Rider

Handbook for the Soul *A collection of wisdom from 30 celebrated spiritual writers*. Piatkus

The Hero with a Thousand Faces *An examination, through ancient myths, of man's eternal struggle for identity,* Joseph Campbell. Fontana Press

How to Know God *The Soul's Journey into the Mystery of Mysteries*, Deepak Chopra. Rider

Jesus and the Lost Goddess *The Secret Teachings of the Original Christians*, Timothy Freke & Peter Gandy. Three Rivers Press

The Journey Home *The Obstacles to Peace*, Kenneth Wapnick. Foundation for A Course In Miracles

The Mysteries *Rudolf Steiner's writings on Spiritual Initiation*, Andrew Welburn. Floris Books

Mysticism *The Nature and Development of Spiritual Consciousness,* Evelyn Underhill. Oneworld

Nine Faces of Christ *Quest of the True Initiate*, Eugene Whitworth. DeVorss

No Destination *Autobiography (of a pilgrimage), Satish Kumar*. Green Books

Pilgrimage *Adventures of the Spirit*, Various Authors. Travellers' Tales

Paths of the Christian Mysteries *From Compostela to the New World*, Virginia Sease and Manfred Schmidt-Brabant. Temple Lodge

The Pilgrimage *A Contemporary Quest for Ancient Wisdom*. Paulo Coelho

Peace Pilgrim *Her Life and Work* Friends of Peace Pilgrim. Ocean Tree Books

Pilgrim in Aquarius David Spangler. Findhorn Press

Pilgrim Stories *On and Off the Road to Santiago*. Nancy Louise Frey. University of California Press.

Pilgrim in Time *Mindful Journeys to Encounter the Sacred*. Rosanne Keller.

The Power of Now *A Guide to Spiritual Enlightenment*. Eckhart Tolle. Hodder & Stroughton.

Peace is Every Step *The path of mindfulness in everyday life*, Thich Nhat Hanh.

Phases *The Spiritual Rhythms in Adult Life*, Bernard Lievegoed. Sophia Books

Sacred Contracts *Awakening Your Divine Potential*, Caroline Myss. Bantam

Sacred Roads *Adventures from the Pilgrimage Trail*, Nicholas Shrady. Viking

Silence of the Heart *Dialogues with Robert Adams*. Acropolis Books

The Art of Pilgrimage *The Seeker's Guide to Making Travel Sacred*, Phil Cousineau. Element Books

The Inner Camino *Path of Awakening through our Intuitive Consciousness*, Sara Hollwey & Jill Brierley. Kaminn Media.

The Prophet. Kahlil Gibran. Mandarin

The Reappearance of the Christ. Alice Bailey. Lucis Press.

The Road Less Travelled *A new Psychology of Love*, M. Scott Peck. Arrow

The Soul's Code *In Search of Character and Calling*, James Hillman. Bantam

RETURNING HOME: *Reflections ...*

When, after a prolonged absence, friends and family remark, *'you haven't changed at all'* I am hopeful they are either blind or following some meaningless social convention. I have spent the last 30 years of my life with the primary intention to do just that – change myself! One of the more potent aspects of pilgrimage is the extended time it requires away from the familiar. This allows an opportunity for the inner alchemy of spirit to start its work of transformation. It's not just the physical body that may need to sweat off excess baggage – the mind needs purifying too. Our world is in a mess and we are not going to fix it with more of the same. We need a fresh approach and a different mind-set to the one that created the chaos in the first place. Hopefully, this re-ordering of the way we see the world will quicken apace as we open to lessons presented to us along the camino and begin to understand that *life itself is the classroom.*

A purpose of pilgrimage is to allow time for old belief systems and outworn 'truths' to fall away so that new and higher perspectives can arise. We may also need to recognise that colleagues and partners at home or at work may feel threatened by our new outlook on life. Breaking tribal patterns, challenging or querying consensus reality is generally considered inappropriate at best or heretical at worst. The extent to which we hold onto any new understanding is measured by how far we are prepared to *walk our talk* and live our 'new' truth in the face of opposition, often from those who profess to love us.

These guidebooks are dedicated to awakening beyond human consciousness. They arose out of a personal existential crisis and the urgent need for some space and time to reflect on the purpose of life and its direction. Collectively we live in a spiritual vacuum of our own making where the mystical and sacred have been relegated to the delusional or escapist. Accordingly, we live in a three dimensional world and refuse to open the door to higher dimensions of reality. We have impoverished ourselves in the process, severely limiting our potential. Terrorised by the chaotic world we have manifested around us, we have become ensnared in its dark forms. We have become so preoccupied with these fearful images we fail to notice that we hold the key to the door of our self-made prison. We can walk out any time we choose.

Whatever our individual experiences, it is likely that we will be in a heightened state of sensitivity after walking the camino. We should avoid squeezing our itinerary or feeling pressurised to rush back into our 'normal life' immediately on our return. This is a crucial moment. I have often witnessed profound change, in myself and others, only to allow a sceptical audience to induce fear and doubt so that we fall back to the relative comfort of our default position, the status quo. Be careful with whom you share your experiences and stay in contact with fellow pilgrims who can support new realisations and orientation. Source new friends and activities that enhance and encourage the on-going journey of Self-discovery.

If you feel it might be helpful, please feel free to email *jb@caminoguides.com* I cannot promise to answer all emails in writing but be assured they will all be noted and a blessing sent in return. I have developed great empathy and respect for my fellow pilgrims who have placed themselves on the path of enquiry. We are embarking together on a journey of re-discovery of our essential nature and opening up to knowledge of Higher Worlds. We have, collectively, been asleep a long time and while change can happen in the twinkling of an eye it is often experienced as a slow and painful process. It is never easy to let go of the familiar and to step into the new. How far we are prepared to go and how resolute in holding onto our new-found reality is a matter of our own choosing. There is little point in garnering peace and understanding along the camino, if we leave it behind in Santiago. We need to bring them back into our everyday life. After the camino comes the laundry!

Whichever choice you make will doubtless be right for you at this time. I wish you well in your search for truth and your journey Home and extend my humble blessings to a fellow pilgrim on the path. The journey is not over and continues, as we will have it be, dedicated to the sacred or the mundane, to waking or sleeping. To help remind us of our true identity, I leave you with the words of Marianne Williamson, often attributed to Nelson Mandela, but distilled from A Course In Miracles and published in A Return to Love.

Our deepest fear is not that we are inadequate.
Our deepest fear is that we are powerful beyond measure.
It is our Light, not our darkness, that most frightens us.

We ask ourselves, who am I to be brilliant, gorgeous, talented
and fabulous?
Actually, who are you not to be? You are a child of God.
Your playing small doesn't serve the world.
There's nothing enlightened about shrinking,
So that other people won't feel insecure around you.

We were born to make manifest the Glory of God that is within us.
It's not just in some of us; it's in everyone.
And as we let our Light shine,
We unconsciously give other people permission to do the same.
As we are liberated from our own fear,
Our presence automatically liberates others.

Before a new chapter is begun, the old one has to be finished.
Stop being who you were, and change into who you are.
Paulo Coelho

A tithe of all royalties from the sale of this guidebook will be distributed to those who seek to preserve the physical and spiritual integrity of this route

12 Caminos de Santiago

❶ Camino Francés 778 km
St. Jean – Santiago
Camino Invierno
Ponferrada – Santiago **275** km

❷ Chemin de **Paris 1000** km
Paris – St. Jean via Tours

❸ Chemin de **Vézelay 900** km
Vezélay – St. Jean via Bazas

❹ Chemin du **Puy 740** km
Le Puy-en-Velay – St. Jean
Ext. to Geneva, Budapest

❺ Chemin d'**Arles 750** km
Arles – Somport Pass
Camino Aragonés **160** km
Somport Pass – Óbanos
Camí San Jaume **600** km
Port de Selva – Jaca
Camino del Piamonte **515** km
Narbonne - Lourdes - St. Jean

❻ Camino de Madrid 320 km
Madrid – Sahagún
Camino de **Levante 900** km
Valencia – Zamora
Alt. via Cuenca – Burgos

❼ Camino Mozárabe 390 km
Granada – Mérida
(Málaga alt. via Baena)

❽ Via de la **Plata 1,000** km
Seville – Santiago
Camino Sanabrés Ourense **110** km

❾ Camino Portugués *Central* **640** km
Lisboa – Porto 389 km
Porto – Santiago 251 km
Camino Portugués *Costa* **320** km
Porto – Santiago
via Caminha & Variante Espiritual

❿ Camino Finisterre 86 km
Santiago – Finisterre
via – Muxía – Santiago **114** km

⓫ Camino Inglés 120 km
Ferrol – Santiago

⓬ Camino del Norte 830 km
Irún – Santiago via Gijón
Camino Primitivo 320 km
Oviedo – Lugo – Melide